# DAY BY DAY
## With Life Coach
### Marlon Lock

EVERYTHING WE TOUCH TURNS TO GOLD

**Day By Day with Life Coach Marlon Lock**

Copyright © 2019 Marlon Lock

All rights reserved. No part of this book may be reproduced or transmitted in any form or by any means, electronic or mechanical, including photocopying, recording, or by any information storage and retrieval system without the written permission of the author or publisher, except where permitted by law.

ISBN: 978-1-949176-25-4 (paperback)

Edited by: Tecia Sellers
Exterior cover design by: Money Graphics LLC

Published by: KRL Publishing


More about the author: www.marlonlock.com.

# INTRODUCTION

My name is Marlon Lock. There is a lot you do not know about me but in the next 365 days you will find out. For starters, I am a husband, a father, a pastor and a certified life coach. I am also a former police officer and beautician (I know right); that's me. I've never regarded myself as an author but here I am.

This book is for you! I ask that you commit to reading every day, one day at a time. If that seems impossible, then I would ask that you get an accountability partner to read this book day-by-day with. This is not a race to see how fast you can read it, but it's a journey.

Get ready to go on a 365-day ride with me. In less than 5 minutes a day you will receive information that will fuel you to your next level. Now I have to tell you this, this book is filled with lots of emotion, passion, and of course, my personality. This book is not about me being right or politically correct, it's about me being me. I tried being someone else, and it didn't work. So, I decided to just be who I am. My advice is to use this book as a tool. Make it a part of your morning routine to plant positivity and seeds of growth into your life. It is a book filled with 365 days of affirmations. Commit to the journey and watch how your life begins to transform.

Are you ready?

Let's begin...

# DAY BY DAY
## With Life Coach
## Marlon Lock

## DAY 1:
## SET A GOAL AND GET IT DONE!

You can do it and just know, I am with you the entire way!

In life we often start out to accomplish whatever goal that may be set before us or goals that we've set for ourselves. Some goals may be identified as finishing school, losing weight, finding a church home, or rededicating your life back to what truly matters. Whatever you are deciding to do just make sure you get it done! This is the first day of the best year of your life! Every day I will be here to help you make it to the next. You got this! Now let's get to work!

**TAKEAWAY:** A goal is great. A plan to achieve the goal is even better.

#OGHBYRG

## DAY 2: FRIEND VS FOE (KNOW THE DIFFERENCE)

Come on this journey with me. It's never too late to start. I was up at 5 am accomplishing goals. I realize that in life when we set a goal, we need to make it public. Why? Because public goals hold you accountable. The same way you set goals in hope to succeed, there will be people that set goals to make you fail. While on this day-by-day journey, quickly find out who's a friend and who's a foe. I am a firm believer in loving everyone, but I also believe in staying away from foes. You got this! See you tomorrow.

**TAKEAWAY:** Stay away from anything that looks wrong (evil).

#OGHBYRG

## DAY 3: DISTRACTION, YOU WILL NOT DISTRACT ME!

I've learned in life that no matter where you are or what you are doing, distractions will come. They will come from family, friends, loved ones, coworkers, loss and even from gain. Be careful not to let the distractions keep you from what you committed to doing. Tell the distraction, "you will not distract me," just like that! Say it until you've completed your assignment for today. What's your assignment you ask?

Spending time with God

Studying

Working out

Choosing healthy eating options

Spending time with family

Allowing yourself to laugh

Choosing to have "good vibes everyday"

**TAKEAWAY:** Whatever you decided for yourself this year don't you let no distraction distract you! Now get to it, we got work to do!

#OGHBYRG

## DAY 4: INSPECT WHAT YOU ARE EXPECTING

I've learned over the years that it's easy to expect something, but true success comes when you inspect it. Let's look deeper. You can expect employees to be on time, do their jobs effectively, not take longer breaks than they're supposed to, and care about the business and the product like the owner does. The reality is that if you don't inspect it, you will end up with less than what you expected! So, don't just assume that all is well but be intentional about inspecting what you expect in every area of your life.

**TAKEAWAY:** Take 10 minutes to write down your expectations (be realistic) then take another 10 minutes and inspect if you are doing the right things to get what you expect. You got this!

#OGHBYRG

## DAY 5:
## DON'T YOU DARE LOSE FOCUS!

The end of the week is tricky because the old you would like to unwind, but don't unwind your focus! Work like today is Monday. Don't just coast because it's the weekend. Go hard like your life depends on it! Why? Because it does!

**TAKEAWAY:** You are on a 365-day journey and you have so many goals and so many people depending on you to reach those goals this year! Don't you dare think about taking a break. You'll break when you can afford to. Now go get it!

#OGHBYRG

## DAY 6: TOO CLOSE TO TURN BACK NOW!

We fall, we get back up!

We laugh, we cry!

We understand some things, and other things we don't! We do a lot of things, but one thing team #OGHBYRG will not do is quit. We don't quit! Welcome to the family!

Obey

God

He'll

Bless

You

Real

Good

Say this out loud so you can hear yourself: "I will finish strong!"

**TAKEAWAY:** You've come too far in these first 5 days to slip up now. We are going to finish, and we are going to finish strong!

#OGHBYRG

# DAY 7: FINISH

Finish this week on a high note that will take you into next week with a drive and commitment.

For me, my high note at the end of every week is going to church. Everyone knows my belief in Jesus Christ as my Lord and Savior and He is what keeps me sane! I couldn't have made it through the week without Him (you either). So, to really end this first seven days and get ready for the next, do something that motivates you and finish strong! See you tomorrow.

**TAKEAWAY:** Reward yourself by ending this week on a high note! Go see a movie, spend time with family, read a book, go to church, do something. You've made it this far. Yes, it's only 7 days but you must get to 7 before you can get to 70.

#OGHBYRG

## DAY 8: WHAT YOU GONE DO?

The sacrifices you made last week made you better for this week. Your thought process was better, you ate healthier, you spent more time with your family, you went to church, you felt better, you were better! Now this week will be even better than last week! Get ready to have the best week of your life!

I am with you all the way.

**TAKEAWAY:** What are you going to do today? I know, be great! See you tomorrow.

#OGHBYRG

## DAY 9: STEP OUTSIDE OF THE FRAME!

Don't get discouraged because your progress may seem a bit slow, it's a journey. Remember the big picture! What's the big picture? It's where you are headed, not where you are! You're not doing what you're doing for people, it's for you! If you are doing it for people, then quit right now! Why? Because you can't please others! Think about how much better everything you are connected with will become, because you didn't give up on your goals and you stepped outside of the frame. I am with you all the way, your friend, Marlon.

**TAKEAWAY:** Go find a picture of you right now and look at. You look good; but just think about how much better you're going to look after you smash all your goals!

#OGHBYRG

## DAY 10: NO MORE EXCUSES!

No more excuses family. Mark Twain said, *"There are thousands of excuses for failure but never a good reason."* That's so powerful! Today I am here right now to pull you from *"someday island."* You've gotten way too comfortable here and it's hurting you! Think of something that you've been putting off for "someday," and do it today.

**TAKEAWAY:** Brian Tracy says, *"Get off of someday island."* Tomorrow is not promised. Don't put off what you can accomplish today for tomorrow.

#OGHBYRG

## DAY 11: IT'S THAT SERIOUS!

Participate in your own success! Don't make excuses, make progress! I had a half of a brownie and nobody knew but me and the Lord, but I knew better. See I am expecting extreme results in every area of my life! So yes, it was, *"that serious."* Until you get to that point where your life goals are *"that serious,"* you will never reach them!

God is that serious

Family is that serious

Health is that serious

Finances are that serious

Your goals are that serious

Over delivering is that serious

**TAKEAWAY:** Stay away from the brownies!

#OGHBYRG

## DAY 12: BE CONSISTENT!

*"Motivation gets you going but discipline keeps you growing."*

I need you to stay focused and committed to your dreams! Your delay is not a denial. Thank you, John Maxwell. You changed my life.

There is no expiration date on your dreams! Why? Because dreams never expire! Chad "C-Note" Roper, thank you for helping me dream again.

Don't you dare relax and become complacent. You are oh so close to your dream! It is so and so it is.

**TAKEAWAY:** The law of consistency says, "Motivation gets you going but discipline keeps you growing."

#OGHBYRG

## DAY 13: IT'S ALL ABOUT YOU!

That's right family, it's all about you. If you are not right, then everything connected with you will not be right!

We spend so much time trying to please others but never take the time to make ourselves happy. You have the right to be happy! This journey you are on now is the best decision that you could have made for you! The same ones talking, are still going to be talking after you exceed your goals. Let'em talk

**TAKEAWAY:** If you are willing to take on other people's opinions about you, be willing to take on their lifestyle as well.

I love y'all family. Success looks good on you.

#OGHBYRG

## DAY 14:
## HAVE A SENSE OF URGENCY

I need you to have a sense of urgency in changing your life and everything connected to you now! In order to get something you've never had, you must do something you've never done!

Be intentional – growth in any area doesn't just happen. That little extra push that I needed was Jesus. Jesus got me over the hump! Now I can't speak for what will get you over, but whatever it may be, you need a sense of urgency about getting it!

**TAKEAWAY:** Get up, get out, and get it done!

#OGHBYRG

## DAY 15: REMEMBER THOSE WHO SERVE

To all our past, present, and future military personnel we thank you! Words can't express how much you are loved and appreciated.

Sometimes we can forget the things that really matter. Things such as having hot water, food, a bathroom, just basic everyday things we take for granted.

But on today take the time to appreciate the small things as well as the things that may seem small but are huge! Like our military. Each day we have someone fighting for us so that we do not have to fight. They allow us to live a safe, peaceful life! To anyone who has served, is serving, or plans on serving our country, thank you! May God keep and cover you in Jesus's name!

**TAKEAWAY:** Find someone who serves or has served our country and buy them lunch, a cup of coffee or at least give them a, "thank you."

#OGHBYRG

## DAY 16: BE INTENTIONAL! GROWTH DOESN'T JUST HAPPEN!

I have made this statement a few times and it is critical that you get it. Whatever your hopes or dreams may be, you can reach them, but you must be intentional during the entire process. If you want to be a better parent, friend, spouse, minister, pastor, business owner, better in weight loss, etc., you must be deliberate in getting better results.

Today right down one thing that must happen in the next 30 days, be intentional on getting it done, and you will get it done. Do you know why? Because you got me all in your ear pushing you! If you do not want to be better in every area of your life... stop reading this book! I challenge you to remain true to the course. We will do some amazing things together.

**TAKEAWAY:** Continue to be intentional.

#OGHBYRG

## DAY 17: BE AWARE OF WHO YOU ARE!

*"You must know yourself to grow yourself." – John Maxwell*

James Russell Lowell said, "No one can produce great things who is not thoroughly sincere in dealing with himself."

Today is all about truly knowing what you have inside of you! I know there's a winner in you, but I need for you to know that as well! Never allow someone else's opinion to become your reality. Walk with purpose and get it done today! Whatever you need to get done, do it!

**TAKEAWAY:** John Maxwell says to, "surround yourself with the thinking that outthinks you."

#OGHBYRG

## DAY 18: TRUST THE PROCESS

A process is the action of going forward or moving on.

This is what I need from you on today. I need you to keep moving in the right direction. If you are going after a goal for others, then you may as well quit right now. Why quit? Your results will not last. You will not remain true to it, if it is not something that you desire; but if what you're doing is for you, regardless if others support you or not, you still will reach your desired goal!

For me, my biggest opponent looks at me in the mirror every day!

The winner within me tells the loser mentality, *"You will not stop me today and you won't stop me tomorrow!"* What's in you? I know. It's passion! That passion gives you energy and that energy is going to make you crush your goals today! Now get up and go get it.

**TAKEAWAY:** Be great!

#OGHBYRG

## DAY 19: ARE YOU A WINNER OR WHINER?

If you are a winner, then you'll take action and respond to adversity. If you are a whiner, then you'll continue to make excuses. Days, weeks, months and years will go by and you'll still be in the same position.

Whining sounds something like this:

Nobody will hire me

I can't lose the weight

I am too young

I am too old

I am not educated enough

They do not care for me (who is they), the devil is a lie! You got me in your life (by way of this book) for a reason! If you do not want to be pushed into your destiny or to that next level, please stop reading; however, if you stay on this journey with me and look in the mirror and talk to that winner inside of you, not only will you win today, but every day.

**TAKEAWAY:** Go dominate!

#OGHBYRG

## DAY 20:
# DO WHAT YOU'VE NEVER DONE TO GET WHAT YOU'VE NEVER HAD.

In order to get something you've never had, you must do something you've never done! I am pushing you towards greatness! Whether you like it or not, you got better coming!

Want to know how I know? I'll explain. I was the guy that always made excuses, always took shortcuts, and then complained when I didn't get committed results. I got results, but you could tell that I took short cuts. Once I decided to do what I'd never done, I ended up with things that I never had. If I can do it, you can do it as well.

**TAKEAWAY:** *"Get 'er done!"* See you tomorrow.

#OGHBYRG

## DAY 21: THE LAW OF CONSISTENCY.

*"Motivation gets you going- discipline keeps you growing."*
*– John Maxwell*

I read somewhere that it takes 21 straight days for anything to become a habit. Guess what? You have been consistent for 21 days. Now there is no stopping you! You will get through this year better than any year of your life!

**TAKEAWAY:** Congratulations! As a reward for what you have done, do something nice (a random act of kindness) for someone else today, expecting nothing in return. What happens after that will blow your mind.

#OGHBYRG

## DAY 22: GET TO THE RIGHT PLACE!

The law of environment says, *"growth thrives in conducive surroundings."*

Check your surroundings today. Check your team that you're connected with. Evaluate and make the necessary changes or non-changes. Keep in mind, it's not always others, it just may be self.

**TAKEAWAY:** Do not let crab mentality people pull you down. If you are "Positive Peter" and *"Negative Nancy"* shows up, here's what you do, go the other way. Protect your peace.

#OGHBYRG

## DAY 23: HELLO FEAR!

Fear makes the wolf bigger than it really is. On today choose not to fear. No weapon formed against you will prosper!

Take fear head on. Look into its eyes, size it up, give it a head nod, and keep it moving. Just make sure when it looks back at you, you say, "Hello, I'm good."

Yes, the weapon has formed!

Yes, you can see it!

You must face it! With hands sweating and knees shaking, you will reach and exceed your goals! Once you crush adversity today, please tell fear thank you for the push!

**TAKEAWAY:** Isaiah 54:17 says, *"No weapon that is formed against thee shall prosper ..."*

#OGHBYRG

## DAY 24: TURN YOUR NEGATIVES INTO POSITIVES.

How do we do this? Be willing to step outside of your comfort zone. If you want an *"average life,"* well then do like everyone else and live like everyone else, and that's cool. But if you want an amazing life then you need to put forth some amazing effort and make all negatives turn into positives! It's a mind-set...

You are comfortable with:

- everyone liking you
- everyone supporting you
- everyone patting you on the back

But what about when:

- they do not like you and tell you
- they do not support on purpose
- they are stabbing you in the back instead of patting you on the back

Regardless of the response, keep pushing.

**TAKEAWAY:** Get uncomfortable! Growth & comfort do not work well together. If you are growing, then you're uncomfortable and if you're comfortable then you're not growing.

#OGHBYRG

## DAY 25: LEAD YOURSELF FIRST THEN OTHERS.

Your greatest leadership challenge will always be self. Be careful not to lead others publicly but not lead self privately. It's not what people see that affects you, it's what they do not see. Andrew Carnegie says, "As I grow older, I pay less attention to what men say. I just watch what they do."

I challenge you today to go look in the mirror at self and make sure you are keeping yourself accountable. It's day 25 and you still got some deadlines to meet, some calls to make, and some emails to go through.

Do it! Lead by example. Have a blessed day!

**TAKEAWAY:** Go be great in all areas today because somebody's watching.

#OGHBYRG

## DAY 26: BEFORE YOU SAY "I QUIT..."

You've already beat the odds because you've made it this far!

- in your walk with Christ
- in your marriage
- on your job
- on a healthier lifestyle
- in decision making
- in better choices

Before you say, *"I quit,"* don't quit!

**TAKEAWAY:** Look at how far you've come in such a short amount of time! Don't you dare let complacency sit next to you! You've made progress, but you still got so much work to do.

#OGHBYRG

## DAY 27: TRUE FRIENDS!

Friend is a word that is used so loosely in society today, but it is truly amazing to have true friends.

One of my favorite passages in the Bible was about a paralyzed man whose friends took him to Jesus in his bed. They couldn't get to Jesus because of the crowd so they took drastic measures and climbed the roof and lowered him down. Those were true friends.

Make sure you have people in your life that by any means necessary, they want to see you better. That's a *"true friend."*

**TAKEAWAY:** When Jesus saw the friends' effort, the paralyzed man got the results.

#OGHBYRG

## DAY 28: IT'S THE SMALL THINGS

*"Small hinges open big doors!"*

To get to that next level you must do the small detailed things that most people won't do. You can do it and you got me pushing you every step of the way!

Every mansion is laid brick by brick.

Every beautiful physique was made repetition by repetition.

Every great team started with one person at a time. Do not skip the process, trust it.

**TAKEAWAY:** I've often heard, *"Do not sweat the small stuff."* But I say, *"Sweat the small stuff."* Everything great started off small. The Bible says, *"Do not despise small beginnings."* Zechariah 4:10

#OGHBYRG

## DAY 29: NOT IN CONTROL

When I lost my mother-in-law it really affected me in so many ways. Not because I hadn't experienced the loss of a loved one. I mean I lost my dad at age 11, I lost both my dad's parents in my thirties, I lost my mother's mom as well in my late 30's. My wife and I even lost a child in the womb. But to be with my mother-in-law riding rides at a water park, then to see her praising God on that Sunday, the day before she died, like never before, only to find her lifeless in her home the next day was mind blowing. It became instantly clear that we are not in total control, God is. The only thing we can control is the choices we make. Make the right choice today to be better than you were on yesterday.

**TAKEAWAY:** You can't control what happens, but you can control how you respond.

#OGHBYRG

## DAY 30: WINNERS WIN!

In life things happen. You can either make an excuse not to get it done or use it to motivate you! Allow what you can't do to propel you to a level where you can do what you thought you couldn't and more!

I know it's in you and you got me to bring it out of you.

We fight

We cry

We laugh

We fall down

We get back up

We finish

We start over

We struggle

We maintain

We succeed

We listen

Most importantly

We win

**TAKEAWAY:** We may fall down 7 times, but by the time we get to 8, you will see us standing.

#OGHBYRG

## DAY 31: OUT WORK EVERYBODY!

Ok so they are better than you.

They may have a bachelor's degree, but you may have an associate degree. You may not have a degree at all.

They may be stronger, faster, and bigger, but this is how you defeat *"them."* Out work them! Be disciplined. Invest in you. It starts at home and it starts now!

*"The harder you work, the harder it is to surrender."* – Vince Lombardi

**TAKEAWAY:** Today remove the word quit from your vocabulary

#OGHBYRG

## DAY 32: BE RESPONSIBLE!

We live in a society where it seems easier to blame others and make excuses, than to take accountability for our own behavior. Be careful not to fall into that trap. Be responsible. That's right! Step up to the plate and do right.

Do right:

By your family.

By your friends.

By your commitments.

By your ministry.

By your community.

By your neighborhood.

In other words, be responsible.

Take the action step and make it happen.

**TAKEAWAY:** Being responsible is the willingness to do what you need to do at the time it needs to be done.

#OGHBYRG

# DAY 33: PREPARE!

*"If I fail to prepare then I am preparing to fail."*

Act today and prepare. Do not just go through life and take what comes. Prepare for life and go after what you really want!

Preparing today will allow you to walk through an upcoming door in your future. Think about everything and everyone depending on you to be prepared.

You can do this, and I am with you every step of the way.

**TAKEAWAY:** I'd rather be prepared, and the door not open than for the door to open and I am not prepared.

#OGHBYRG

## DAY 34: HAPPY FATHER'S DAY!

We as dads carry a lot all day, every day. Sometimes we seem to get the short end of the stick. Today I want to recognize all the dads.

If you are not doing your part, you have it in you to be a better dad. Find you a great church to learn some biblical principles, then find a great dad to mentor you on how to become one.

Now you're probably saying today isn't Father's Day, but I beg to differ. Every day is Father's Day! Your child is depending on you each day to be the best dad you can be.

I am with you every step of the way.

**TAKEAWAY:** Contact a dad today and let them know how proud you are of them. Trust me, this will go a long way.

#OGHBYRG

## DAY 35: KEEP IT MOVING!

Whatever life brings, accept the challenge, look to God for strength, and keep it moving!

You will have moments where you become frustrated and feel as if you're all alone. Just know that you are not. You would be surprised at how many people you have rooting for you!

You can do it and just know I am with you along this journey called *"life."*

**TAKEAWAY:** It set you back, now keep it moving.

#OGHBYRG

# DAY 36: MAKE GOOD DECISIONS!

Make sure you can live with the choices you make today, for the rest of your life. Yes, it's that's serious!

Many times, we take the path of least resistance not realizing that it will cause you pleasure at first but great pain in the future. So be wise, seek counsel, and never make a permanent decision based on a temporary situation.

**TAKEAWAY:** My granddad would always say, "Son if you make your bed hard, be willing to lay in it."

#OGHBYRG

## DAY 37: MAKE THE DECISION.

*"It's not that we do not know what the right decision is, it's just that we must make it."* – John Maxwell

The *"right"* decision may be unpopular, confrontational, indecisive and fearful. But guess what? You still must make it. Put your big boy/big girl pants on and do what needs to be done. Ask God to go before you and speak through you on the toughest decisions and discussions you'll have to make in life.

I am with you every step of the way.

Your friend, Marlon.

**TAKEAWAY:** One of my favorite scriptures in the Bible is Proverbs 3:6, *"In all thy ways acknowledge him and he shall direct thy paths."*

#OGHBYRG

# DAY 38: THE JOURNEY

On June 23, 1981, I was chosen by God to preach the gospel of Jesus Christ (my Lord and Savior). Being chosen at a young age came with many challenges. Like most, I strayed away to *"do me,"* only to realize that *"doing me"* was the worst thing to do. I then decided to go back and *"do Jesus."* Let me tell you, my life has changed for the better. I am not saying everyday is easy because it's not. I am not saying that I do not miss loved ones that have passed on because I do; but what I am saying is that with God, it is so much easier to deal with life. The peace that I now have, I wouldn't trade it for nothing in the world!

God, thank you for choosing me. I promise to represent you the right way and give you all the honor and the praise! Go ahead and do what you wanna do. I am ready now.

Guess what, that goes for you as well! Don't stress over the journey. The journey is what makes the destination fun.

**TAKEAWAY:** Do like I did and let God do what He wants to do in your life! Enjoy the journey. Test and trials only come to make you strong.

#OGHBYRG

## DAY 39: HAVE THE RIGHT ATTITUDE!

The law of the bad apple says, *"Rotten attitudes ruin a team."* – John Maxwell

You and your team should be crushing everything! Y'all got the talent, the ambition, all the right people, but instead of dominating you all are self-destructing.

If you feel like this, you need to get out of this rut immediately. Wrong vibes are just that...wrong!

Disconnect from it before it destroys your team and your peace. To all Pastors, business owners, teachers, law enforcements, fire departments, schools, and coaches – contact me if you need help in this area. I would love to provide my services to help your team win!

**TAKEAWAY:** I used to think it was everyone else, but when I changed my attitude, I realized that it was me.

#OGHBYRG

## DAY 40: DO NOT TAKE IT FOR GRANTED!

This is the day that the Lord has made. Do not take it for granted!

What if you only had 5 minutes left to enjoy the ones you love the most? Newsflash: We do not know how much time we have left with them. Enjoy your family. Enjoy your loved ones. Enjoy your friendships. Enjoy while you can. Talk about the not so good, patch things up and move forward. As upset as you may want to be, it would crush you if that person was gone. Do not let this opportunity pass you by.

**TAKEAWAY:** Reach out to someone that you love but have become disconnected from. Tell them how much they mean to you and that you just wanted to let them know. Now take 10 seconds of courage and go do it.

#OGHBYRG

## DAY 41: WALK IN YOUR PURPOSE.

I just stopped by to let you know that you are needed, and your life has a purpose! You may have messed up or have gotten off track, but today I am giving you permission to forgive yourself and walk in your purpose! Yes permission!!!

Your past mistakes have given you permission to think that you do not deserve better. I am giving you permission to know your better is on its way! As a matter of fact, your better is here, but you have to let go of what you did, or others did to you in the past. Set up a meeting today and introduce your passion to your purpose. Let them go out on a date, fall in love, and get married!

You ain't seen nothing yet! Walk in your purpose.

**TAKEAWAY:** When your purpose meets your passion, look out! There will definitely be an explosion!!!

#OGHBYRG

# DAY 42: WHO ARE YOU?

It's easy to say who we are but if we take a good look in the mirror, we may not be the person we say that we are.

Here's what we're going to do. Let's reintroduce ourselves to ourselves and begin today to be the best person we can be, without thinking of others, okay? This may seem selfish but let's be honest, you need to be the best you before you can truly help someone else be the best them.

Do it family. Today!

**TAKEAWAY:** The law of the mirror says, "See value in yourself to add value to yourself."- John Maxwell

#OGHBYRG

## DAY 43: BEAUTY IN YOUR BROKENNESS!

You've been blessed by God with gifts whether you use them or not; but you had to be broken so that you wouldn't think that your blessings and giftedness were all about you. Now that you've been broken, you have to totally depend on God.

Think about all the people you will help get through because you went through the process of nurturing and growing yourself to have the capacity to utilize your gifts for the greater good. Get excited about the beauty in your brokenness.

**TAKEAWAY:** Broken crayons still color.

#OGHBYRG

## DAY 44: LET IT GO!

You are holding on to some things that are so heavy that you can't function! Stop trying to be there for everyone else but won't be there for yourself.

Stop carrying around the weight of a grudge that you have against someone. You're missing out on so many present opportunities because you won't let go of the past.

I am challenging you today to simply *"let it go!"*

Yes, they may have did you wrong.

Yes, they may look like they are prospering.

Yes, they lied on you.

But guess what, you still made it through! That's right, through all the bull. And guess what? You will keep making it! Because all you do is win!

**TAKEAWAY:** Go right now and find a mirror. Look at yourself in that mirror and say these words:

All I do is win!

Say it until you mean it.

Say it until you feel it.

Say it until you'll never forget it.

Because that's all you do, you win!

#OGHBYRG

## DAY 45: WHAT IS YOUR WHY?

Why are you doing what you're doing, everyday?

What's the purpose behind it?

Why are you working out?

Why are you in the relationship?

Why did you take the job?

If what you're doing is not stretching you to the max, or if your why doesn't make you cry...

Then it's not big enough!!!!

You got greatness in you... you betta' stop playing!

Now get up and go get what's yours!

**TAKEAWAY:** On your way to reach your why, please know that everybody can't go.

#OGHBYRG

## DAY 46: YES, YOU ADD VALUE TO IT!

Don't trip on the road you may be on now.... why? Because you've just been rerouted!

Yes, God can, He will, and He wants to use someone just like you! Many of you know my testimony or heard the rumors. Some true, some not!

I will say this, God chose me and kept me, even when I didn't want to be kept. The same God is doing the same thing for you!

We oftentimes beat ourselves up over past mistakes that block our ability to dream again for our future.

You are valuable!

To your family

To your job

To your community

To your neighborhood

To everyone you connect with

**TAKEAWAY:** Now go be awesome!

#OGHBYRG

## DAY 47: TEAMWORK DOES MAKE THE DREAM WORK!

I know this sounds cliche but it's true. It was never intended for you go through life alone. Even when you may feel at times you are alone, you're not! Don't ever give way to that negative voice inside of you that wants you to feel alone. In my moments of frustration or loneliness, I love reading the Bible. As you probably can tell, it's my favorite book. One scripture tells me that God gave His son Jesus and that Jesus gave His life for everyone! That's right, for everyone. Not just the good, but everyone. He did this to make us a part of the team! The winning team! Now you may not believe that story and that's your prerogative. All I am saying is, if the team that you're on keeps losing, come join the winning team! The right team gets you in the right places at the right times.

**TAKEAWAY:** Read St. Jonn 3:16. If not a believer, then read St. John 3:16

#OGHBYRG

# DAY 48: WATCH OUT FOR DEATH WORDS.

Don't ever speak anything negative over yourself or anyone else!

*"Life and death are in the power of the tongue."* – Proverbs 18:21

Watch out for speaking *"failure language."* That's right, *"failure language."* What you say is actually what you will get.

Here are some examples:

I am tired – you keep yawning

I am never going to catch up with my bills – you stay behind

I am not good enough – you never get selected

Nobody likes me – nobody likes you

Speak blessings over your life and if someone tries to speak negativity, then politely remove/block them. Use your mouth as a weapon to fight for you not a weapon against you.

**TAKEAWAY:** Write down 5 awesome things about you and say them to yourself out loud every day for the next 10 days.

#OGHBYRG

## DAY 49: SUCCESS IS PREDICTABLE!

Please know that nature doesn't take sides. Nature is neutral. What happens to you is simply a matter of of law. The Law of Cause and Effect – Brian Tracy

3 requirements for success:

1. Decide what you want in life.

2. Determine the price you must pay to get it.

3. Resolve to pay that price.

That's it in a nutshell family! Decide, commit and succeed!

No more excuses! Look at how far you've come. Tomorrow is day 50! Are you kidding me? You've been on this journey for 49 days.

You've lost weight (baggage that you did not need; some stressers that weighed you down).

Your relationships are better.

You're more focused.

You're timelier.

Everything is moving forward in your life all because success is predictable. Keep up the good work and see you tomorrow, day 50!

**TAKEAWAY:** We all have the same 24 hours in a day. What you've been doing in those 24 hours every day, determines where you are right now

#OGHBYRG

## DAY 50: TODAY IS THE DAY!

I read somewhere that the number 50 means the release of debt and burdens. I do not know how you feel, but what we've accomplished these last 50 days has been remarkable. I mean seriously, just look at how far we've come!

These last 50 days we've cleared up some debt, we've mended some relationships, we've lost some weight and threw out some as well...

Now, if you believe that God is about to lift some more burdens and clear some more debt in these next 50 days, I need you to scream loud as you can wherever you may be, *"It is so!"*

**TAKEAWAY:** Go share your 50-day journey with someone that needs a push.

Then go tell your family or accountability partner(s) how much you appreciate them for sticking with you these first 50 days. Finally, go get your favorite dessert and do not share it! You deserve it all!

See you in the morning for day 51.

Ps. These next 50 days are going to blow your mind!

#OGHBYRG

# DAY 51:
## WALK BY FAITH NOT BY SIGHT!

A lot of times we ask God to move. However, we do not experience His movement because we have not "moved" according to His Word.

Faith is present tense which means it works now in the moment you act on what you're hoping for.

The ministry that I attend, we left the church walls and moved. (We walked throughout the neighborhood being a light to those that are in darkness.) What does that mean? All it means is that you have to show people a better way, not just have better talk. We walked by faith expecting God to transform not just the neighborhood but the people that live in the neighborhood.

When we returned from the walk, we experienced power inside the church walls like never before! Jesus still saves. Jesus still heals. Jesus still delivers.

*"And in all the land of your possession ye shall grant a redemption for the land."* – Leviticus 25:24 KJV

**TAKEAWAY:** Step outside of your walls today and do something you've never done. I guarantee you'll get something you've never had.

#OGHBYRG

## DAY 52:
## BE YOU! YOU ARE AWESOME.

Pay close attention. We all have areas where we can improve and should improve, but let's make sure we're doing it for us and not for them. If you're only trying to improve for them, once *"them"* is out the picture, you will be right back to the same old you.

Improve for you and become a better you. Once you get better, everything connected with you gets better.

Enjoy day 52. Do something nice for someone else today that you do not know. Why do this, you may be wondering? Simply because awesome people do awesome stuff!

**TAKEAWAY:** Walk in your awesomeness today. You wear it well.

#OGHBYRG

## DAY 53: YOUR LATTER WILL BE GREATER THAN YOUR FORMER!

Growing up I used to hear this saying all the time in church, and honestly, I had no idea what it meant. As I grew older and wiser, I researched what the seasoned saints were talking about. In the Bible, the book of Job says, *"Though thy beginning was small, yet thy latter end should greatly increase."*

Wow! This gets me so excited because where I started is not where I'll end up! The same goes for you! Where you are on this day, day 53 is not where you'll stay! You're getting stronger, wiser, and better everyday!

Run with this and never forget that you started with little, but you will end with much! Much peace, laughter, patience, empathy, purpose, passion, love, kindness, I could go on.

**TAKEAWAY:** There are so many great things in store for you. Just stay true to the course and watch how awesome it ends up. See ya tomorrow!

#OGHBYRG

## DAY 54: BE GRATEFUL!

You may not see it now, but just know you have something special in you!

Regardless of past mistakes and closed doors... God is still gonna get the glory out of your life.

Be grateful that you woke up this morning.

Be grateful that you can get around without assistance.

Be grateful that you have breath in your lungs.

Be grateful that you got another chance.

Be grateful that you made it through whatever.

So often we take for granted all that we have to be grateful for. I've learned that you don't miss a thing until it's gone. Be grateful.

**TAKEAWAY:** Your situation could be a lot worse! Be grateful!

#OGHBYRG

## DAY 55: DOORS ARE OPENING!

Now in case you haven't noticed by now I am the most optimistic guy you'll ever meet. Why? Because I realized as a young boy that life is all about how I look at a situation that determines how I feel about the situation.

I see a glass with water in it to the middle of the cup as half full not half empty.

I see clouds and rain not as it's gloomy but as God is about to water the earth to feed families.

I see setbacks as tests to make me stronger.

I notice the not so good in people, but I am always looking for the good.

That is why I can tell you today that you have some doors that are opening for you! That's right. I don't care about the doors that were closed in your face or the ones people said you weren't qualified to go in. I am telling you that you, yes you, have some doors that are opening for you soon! If you do not want it to happen then please stop reading this book! If you keep reading and applying what you read… Boom!

**TAKEAWAY:** Say out loud, "Doors are opening for me!"

#OGHBYRG

## DAY 56:
## DON'T TRY TO BE PERFECT BUT ALWAYS BE PASSIONATE!

Be careful not to miss out on an opportunity waiting for the perfect time or perfect situation. That *"perfection"* doesn't exist. The only perfect timing is when you mix your faith with the effort.

John Maxwell says, *"The "perfection gap" says – I have to find the best way before I start."*

No, you don't!

I know you don't want to mess up!

I know you think you're not good enough!

I know there are others more qualified!

But guess what else I know... nobody has the passion and fire that you have! That's right nobody!

Get in that room that you feel you don't belong in and knock their socks off! Make them hire you! Make them call you back! Make them give you a raise! Let your passion ignite the room! Show them your fearlessness! When you get knocked on the face say, *"May I have another!"* When they tell you to go through a brick wall ask, "How many times?"

Hey, opportunities are there! Go get it!

**TAKEAWAY:** *"If you ever see me and a bear in a dark alley.... Help the bear!"* – Michael Lock

# DAY 57: BE HONEST!

So, I was out of town to sing, and I love going to the best mall in every city that I visit. It's retail therapy, right? While walking into the mall a guy named Freddy asked for some money but showed me his sign that said, *"It's for beer."* Although I didn't give him money, I loved his personality and honesty. We all can learn a lot from Freddy.

I didn't judge him and if he wanted food I would've got him whatever to eat. Freddy was in his own world minding his own business, but he was honest! Honesty goes so far.

You may be up today but down tomorrow. Never look down on anyone unless you're willing to pick them up.

**TAKEAWAY:** If you see Freddy, tell him Marlon Lock says, *"Hello and take care."*

#OGHBYRG

## DAY 58: THE GIFT IS IN YOU!

Just know that you have something incredible in you. It just needs to be stirred up! I was reading a story about a man named Paul in the Bible that had a protégé named Timothy. Timothy was young and timid, but Paul saw the giftedness in Timothy and had to pull it out of him. Paul reminded Timothy of the faith and spiritual foundation laid by his mom and auntie, which instilled all the values and greatness in Timothy. Paul simply told Timothy to, *"Stir up the gift that's in you..."* 2 Timothy 1:6.

I am telling you the same thing on day 58! Stir it up!

Don't be timid!

Don't be afraid because it's in you! Just stir it up!

I don't care how many *"no's"* you've received. Get ready for the *"yes"* that's coming your way. To Rico Love, thanks for the impartation.

And yes, I've turned the lights on!

**TAKEAWAY:** If you go to a buffet restaurant and get macaroni and cheese, always stir it up first or ask the attendant to stir it for you. The good stuff is at the bottom, it just needs to be stirred.

#OGHBYRG

## DAY 59: CREATE YOUR OWN OPPORTUNITY!

It took me some time to learn that nobody is going to give me anything! Success is not given just like respect, it's earned! Stop waiting for a hand out!

Stop looking for a magic pill!

Stop making excuses!

Like Brian Tracy would say, *"Just shut up and do it!"*

Not just with working out, not just in school, not just business, but in everything that you do.

Be grateful, humble and stay hungry! Never get full. Remember if there is no door to walk through... build one! I got some tools if you need some help.

**TAKEAWAY:** Why look for a hand out when you can go fix your own plate? – Marlon Lock

#OGHBYRG

## DAY 60: TAKE THE SHOT!

So many times, we don't go after it.

We complain about where we are and what we're doing but never change. We never take a chance on what could be great. I hear so many people say, *"I am not going to do this forever."* My question to you is, why are you even doing it now?

I knew I wouldn't be working for Master Lock all my life, so I left. I knew I wouldn't be a barber all my life, so I went after another opportunity. I thought I'd be a cop for 25 years then retire, but God had a change of plans.

What I am saying is that you can do or be whatever you want, but you must go for it! Take the shot!

Go ahead and take the shot at your dreams.

Listen, I am giving you the pass right now, time is winding down....

5,4,3,2,1.... take the shot.

**TAKEAWAY:** I took a shot at the prettiest, most sweet lady in the world. I thought: *"No freaking way she will marry me...."*

She did!

#OGHBYRG

## DAY 61: DO IT SECRETLY AND GET REWARDED OPENLY.

You've been grinding and working so hard on your goals. I want you to be excited and happy, but just know that everyone is not going to be happy for you and that's okay.

Learn to keep some stuff to yourself and by next year this time what you've been doing in the dark is going to show in the light.

Keep going, keep grinding and keep growing. You're winning family.

**TAKEAWAY:** My granddad used to say, *"Son, never let your left hand know what your right hand is doing."* That's why hands aren't stuck together.

#OGHBYRG

## DAY 62: BE A PEACEMAKER.

I really looked at myself some years ago on being a peace maker. It is not that I didn't promote peace, but I now find myself looking for problems and finding a way to make it peaceful.

It's so easy to keep something negative going on instead of bringing it to an end.

When someone tells me something negative about a person or situation, I ask them, *"what are you doing to make the situation better?"* I made up in my mind that if I can't help, I will not continue to keep the negative fire burning. Why? Because I can bring peace to any situation.

Will you join me?

**TAKEAWAY:** Follow peace and you won't end up in confusion.

#OGHBYRG

# DAY 63: DON'T GOSSIP!

We all have areas that we need to get better. Let's uplift one another instead tearing each other down.

I know you like juicy stuff! We want the messy things. The messier it is, the more of it we buy in to. Look at reality tv, it's not even reality it's scripted, but we don't care, we love the he say, she say.

Life is way too short to be worrying about other people. If you can't pray for them then don't make matters worse. We can do this family. Instead of gossiping speak positive things into existence.

Speak over your life.

Speak over your marriage.

Speak over your children.

Speak over your finances.

Speak good instead of gossip.

**TAKEAWAY:** If you can't keep from gossiping about others, then take your tongue out.

#OGHBYRG

# DAY 64: BE ON TIME!

Listen family, please take this love that I am giving it. Don't nobody got time to wait around on you. If you have a time to be somewhere then you need to make the necessary steps to be there on time.

Ok that was a bit rough, let me say it in a different tone. Being on time shows respect and relieves stress.

You ever been late to an appointment? Think of the inconvenience you are causing the person waiting on you. Your being late causes them to be late for their next appointment.

Have you ever been late and got stressed out? Yes, you have.

Let's get it together people. As my grandmother would say, *"You know better now do better."*

**TAKEAWAY:** Be 15 minutes early for work and appointments. This will just make life so much easier.

#OGHBYRG

## DAY 65: RECONNECT!

So much can happen in the course of a year. Some good, some not so good. Either way we must realize that life goes on and we still have dreams to chase and goals to accomplish.

So, family I need each of you to reconnect. That's right! Reconnect yourselves back to your passion, your hopes and your dreams.

We are not waiting until next year, we are starting right now! Yes, right now! Why put off for tomorrow what you can do today?

Disconnect from the negative and reconnect with the positive.

**TAKEAWAY:** Get to know yourself again. Sometimes we can get lost in the shuffle with all the noise. Find a quiet place and reconnect.

#OGHBYRG

# DAY 66: GOD DO WHAT YOU WANT TO DO!

As you know, I am a follower of Christ. I don't force my beliefs on anyone, but I do share them with everyone.

While at our youth Bible camp, we let the kids know that God is our redeemer and no matter what the situation is, what it looks or feels like, God can move on their behalf.

I know this from personal experience. Every time I tried to do it my way, it always backfired! I always struggled and got into jams that I seemed to not be able to get out of. Then finally I stopped doing the same things expecting different results. I allowed God to do what he wanted to do in my life!

Now the same God that did it for me and for the children, wants to do it for you!

**TAKEAWAY:** If you can't seem to manage life on your own, get some help. It may not come from a church setting or from a therapist, but it will come from somewhere. You got this!

#OGHBYRG

## DAY 67: LEARN TO SAY "NO."

We often look at the word "no" as something negative when it's not.

As a pastor and just a lover of people, I had to learn not to over exert myself because I try to do it all, be involved in all and help all. But the reality was it was taking away from me in other areas.

Now, do I still love people? Yes.

Will I still be a great human being? Yes.

Will I continue to give God my best? Of course.

But I've learned how and when to say…

No.

Please take this day seriously. You can't be all things to all people, only God can. So, saying no sets boundaries and limitations in all areas of your life.

**TAKEAWAY:** No doesn't mean never.

#OGHBYRG

## DAY 68: SPEAK SOMETHING POSITIVE!

It's so easy to become negative, a *"Negative Nancy."*

Today I want you to speak something positive over your life! Yes! Think about when a child is learning how to walk. Although the child falls repeatedly, we clap and cheer and say things like, *"good job"* or, *"it's ok keep trying you can do it."* Boy does this put a smile on that child's face. But when we get older, when we fall, we get negative comments which can lead us in to a state of depression or anxiety. So, from now on:

Speak over yourself

Encourage yourself

You are great!

**TAKEAWAY:** *"Life and death are in the power of the tongue."*

#OGHBYRG

# DAY 69: THE INVITATION!

I want to invite you to a better life. That's right, I want you to take a chance at something even better. Now it's been 69 days and I know for a fact that you are better in so many areas of your life!

I must at least invite you for an opportunity to an even better life. Okay so here it is, I accepted Jesus Christ as my Lord and Savior and decided to follow His ways. It was the best decision I ever made in my life.

Do I still have problems that arise? Yes.

Do I still have issues to deal with? Yes.

Do I still get tempted? Yes; but having Jesus on my side and in my life makes it so much easier to deal with. This is why I am inviting you to try Jesus as an option. One try will change your life for the better, forever. Your decision will change from Jesus being an option to becoming the source.

**TAKEAWAY:** If your life is grand then keep doing what you're doing. But if you need help, I invite you to give the Lord a try.

#OGHBYRG

# DAY 70: THE 4 C'S

I want to thank a mentor of mines for teaching me this. Not only has this helped me but it has helped everyone that I've taught it to and today it's going to help you.

We often think to accomplish anything we need confidence, but confidence is actually the last thing you get. Let's take a quick look.

The first thing you need to do is commit. Commitment to any goal is the first step.

Then you get courage. Courage comes once you commit and realize you can do it.

Then you get capability. When you get here, it starts to get good.

Finally, confidence comes. Look out because the flood gates are open. You are unstoppable!

**TAKEAWAY:** Make sure you get your alphabet in order... It's not ABCD it's CCCC!

#OGHBYRG

## DAY 71: TEACH AND LEARN!

In life we must teach as well as learn. We must teach from our experiences as well as learn from others.

What are you willing to pass on to another person or another generation? If we don't teach them, how will they know? If they don't know, how can they grow? Today I want you to pass on some knowledge to someone and look to receive some knowledge from another. Never get to a point where you're not willing to take the time and compassion to teach; and never get so uppity that you can't learn.

My daughter will never forget that her grandma took the time to teach and show her with love and patience how to make homemade mashed potatoes and banana nut bread. I think this is pretty cool. I know Nanna is in Heaven smiling that her babies are still learning.

**TAKEAWAY:** When you learn something teach it to someone immediately, this way you will retain what you learned.

#OGHBYRG

## DAY 72: BE A PROBLEM SOLVER.

It's easy to point out what's wrong, but how many of us try to make it right?

In life you will deal with some type of problem every day. The problem is not really the issue, but rather how we go about solving the problem. Just because we don't agree, doesn't mean that we have to be upset to the point where we don't like one another. Let's learn how to sit down at the table, voice our opinions, respect the other person's opinion, and come up with a reasonable solution and move on.

Please stop with the grade school foolery people. We are adults so act like it!

You are on the verge of your biggest breakthrough, about to close a multimillion-dollar deal, but you're going to miss out because you can't resolve small issues.

Let's do better and get what's in store for us by being willing to simply solve the problem.

**TAKEAWAY:** *"True strength is the courage to admit weakness."* – Simon Sinek

#OGHBYRG

## DAY 73: SEE THE VALUE IN YOURSELF!

You fell down, folks laughed at you, criticized you, and made a ditch for you; but they had no idea you would get back up, fill the ditch with water and go swimming.

Get focused! Get back on the grind and just know that you have some doors that God is preparing to open for you. How you get back is based on how you value yourself. You can do failure alone, but success requires a team. Guess what? You have a team of people, #TeamOGHBYRG pushing you on this journey.

I am with you every step of the way. Now let's get to it! You are valuable.

**TAKEAWAY:** You must see it in you before anyone else does.

#OGHBYRG

## DAY 74: LEARN HOW TO BE STILL!

So often we allow the enemy to have us going back and forth with no real sense of direction. Before you know it, life's crazy!

I challenge you today to just be still and let God be in control of your life.

It's a decision that you must make and commit to because that is what will change your life for the better. When we move too fast and too much, we miss out on the simple things. Today's fast-paced society will cause you to miss out on things like birthdays, walks in the park, naps, snowball fights, sunsets...you get the picture.

So slow down and enjoy the peace of God.

When you slow down, the craziness will still be going on.

When you are broke, they'll still be spending without you.

When you are jobless, they'll still be going to work. When you need the ones that got you going back and forth, where will they be? Probably living their lives and leaving you to figure out what you're going to do with yours.

**TAKEAWAY:** Spend one day this week playing a board game with your family.

#OGHBYRG

# DAY 75: I'LL BE RUNNING BACK TO YOU...

In 2016, I released an EP entitled *"Unleashed."* On that EP, I wrote a song called Running Back to You. The song is about a young man that left his home to live the wild life. He got to a point in his life where he lost everything and went back to his father's house.

Is there something that you ran away from that you need to run back to?

We all have fallen at some point in life, in some area. We often don't know how to get back on track. The Bible tells of the prodigal son, who was in this same place - lost and confused in a pig's pen with no hope. The Bible says that he, *"came to himself,"* and went back to his father's house.

Someone reading this needs to come back home, come back to Jesus. Put pride aside, forget about the feeling of embarrassment, and think about how great your life is going to be, all because you ran back to Jesus.

**TAKEAWAY:** Hurry up and get back!

#OGHBYRG

## DAY 76: WE ARE STRONGER TOGETHER.

In life you will have moments where it seems as if nobody understands and you're all alone.

When this happens, if not careful, you'll end up trying to do it all by yourself. Don't fall into this trap!! You need the help of others. God is gonna connect you with the right people.

My one person that keeps me strong is my wife. She is definitely the rock in the relationship. What a blessing to have her in my life.

Connect with someone to help you reach your goals. Remember we are stronger together!

**TAKEAWAY:** It was never intended for you to go at it alone.

#OGHBYRG

## DAY 77: PRAY FOR OUR NATION.

I woke to the news of something that does not surprise me, but it does frustrate me. Racism. Racism is a problem we can't ignore or run away from. It's an issue today, and it has been an issue throughout history.

It reminded me so much of how far we have not come. Especially after seeing the movie Detroit; however, I cannot allow my frustrations to make me act like the enemy wants us all to act.

I encourage you all to do the same. Don't act the way society suggests you do or makes you to be. Jesus told us about this. He said there is spiritual wickedness is high places. He also said that if our gospel is hidden, it is hidden to those who are lost. Family, the enemy sends distractions to hide the gospel.

Remain focused but stand up for truth in righteousness. Remember, other people don't determine your value; God does.

**TAKEAWAY:** Don't see black or white, see the human race.

#OGHBYRG

## DAY 78: THANK YOU!

There is someone that has helped you along the way in some area. I challenge you to reach out to them today and simply tell them *"thank you."* You'd be surprised at how much that would mean to them.

Thank you is used so much, but I am not sure if we realize how valuable thank you is. It shows gratitude and a level of appreciation for those that have done anything for you regardless of how great or small. Close this book and pick up the phone. Call someone and tell them, *"Thank you!"*

**TAKEAWAY:** You didn't make it this far by yourself. Who are you going to thank?

#OGHBYRG

## DAY 79: SUPPORT A CAUSE.

There's always something bigger than you. I realize that you may have your own issues or dilemma but trust me, there's someone that had an issue far worse than yours.

For example, think of those battling cancer, sickle cell, aids, depression, drug addiction, and the list goes on.

Find a cause to support. Find an organization that's doing something to make lives better and join in! Help make someone else's life better.

**TAKEAWAY:** If you don't stand for something then you will fall for anything.

#OGHBYRG

# DAY 80: IMPART

There is someone that needs you. They need you because you have something that they may be missing. You have so much to offer.

Think about...

The fatherless child.

The motherless child.

The homeless person.

The drug addict.

The alcoholic.

The preacher that's gifted but has no structure.

The millionaire that has money but no peace.

The lawyer that wins cases but is dishonest.

A lot of messed up people wear great costumes. What am I saying? Someone needs you to impart into them, others need you to pray for them. Someone just needs you to tell them, *"Everything is ok,"* or *"Good job."*

Now what may seem like nothing at all to you can mean so much to someone else. Reach out and impart some wisdom and knowledge into someone else.

**TAKEAWAY:** Someone helped you. Pay it forward.

#OGHBYRG

# DAY 81: FAITH!

Faith is needed in all areas of life, but faith can be scary. It's a lot easier to go after what you can see. It can be a bit frustrating and scary going after or believing in something you cannot see.

The reality is that we all have some inkling of faith and we don't even recognize it.

The apostles, yes, the ones right next to Jesus, said to Jesus, *"Increase our faith."* They were basically saying, *"We are all kind of struggling with what we don't see or understand."* So my question to you is what's causing your faith to struggle?

I will admit that faith isn't easy for many because they don't realize that faith is action! That's right, faith is not a wish or a hope IN something, it's actually the substance of what you're hoping for.

So, stop hoping for it; activate your faith and claim it!

**TAKEAWAY:** Jesus used a mustard seed to get the disciples' attention. It's not in the quantity of faith, it's in the quality of your faith.

#OGHBYRG

## DAY 82: PRAY FOR OTHERS.

My family and I attended an event in Wisconsin called the Parade of Homes. It's where you can look at brand new homes and their designs to get ideas or even purchase one of the homes. We actually went on the behalf of another family, who had a desire to relocate.

In life you must not just think about yourself, but you must think about others. Always thank God for what you have and believe him for greater!

**TAKEAWAY:** Stop right now and say a prayer for someone. Don't tell them that you prayed for them but just watch how their lives change for the better.

#OGHBYRG

## DAY 83: FIND THE KID IN YOU.

It's so easy to get stuck in the mindset of being a grown up. The problem with this mentality is that you forget how to be a kid – enjoying life.

Remember when you could play all day? You could watch movies all night and still wake up and do it all over again without a care in the world. No matter what happened throughout your day, you knew that everything would be okay.

I am telling you the same thing today, everything is going to be okay. Go back to that *"childlike"* faith. That's where you just trust that everything is alright. As a child you ask for milk and cookies. You ask for video games. You ask for your favorite tennis shoe. You never ask where the money is coming from, you just expect it's going to be provided.

Find that kid in you. Take time to laugh, get dirty in the mud, and play video games. Not all day everyday, but at least once a month do something super fun that you like. The kid inside of you needs it.

**TAKEAWAY:** Call 3 of your closest friends and play a game of tag.

#OGHBYRG

## DAY 84: YOU'RE GONNA MAKE IT!

I need you to say out loud, *"I am gonna make it!!!!"*

I know it may seem strange, but you need to do this! You need to hear you tell yourself that you're going to make it!

I read somewhere that by the time we reach 18 years old we've heard *"no"* thousands of times more than we've heard *"yes."* Guess what this does? It makes us think that no is acceptable and will come often and yes is rare and it'll come sparingly.

Let me help you change the way you think. When "no" is at the front of your brain, it makes you think you can't make it! Yes, you can make it! Say out loud, *"I am going to make it!"*

**TAKEAWAY:** You are the thoughts you think of yourself.

#OGHBYRG

# DAY 85: APOLOGIZE

Life is way too short to be going back and forth trying to have the *"last word."* If you really want the last word, just apologize.

Now I know you think it doesn't make sense when you've been wronged but be the bigger person and apologize.

**TAKEAWAY:** Just be the bigger person and apologize.

#OGHBYRG

# DAY 86: JURY DUTY

So why did I get picked for jury trial?

My wife has never been called! Others I know have NEVER been called. Why choose me?

I was so frustrated sitting in court all day long but then I thought about it. Someone's freedom is at stake. There is a victim hoping that justice is served. Looking at it from this point, it was my duty to do jury trial and help the judicial system make the right choice.

You have a duty as well. That's right, to uphold justice and do your part in society. I am grateful for a country where there's liberty and justice for all.

**TAKEAWAY:** Stop complaining and do your part. If you can't be a part of the solution, then please don't be apart of the problem.

#OGHBYRG

## DAY 87: ENJOY YOUR RELATIONSHIPS.

I have so many people that mean so much to me in my life. Each one brings a different dynamic to the word relationships.

I have my relationship with my wife and my children.

I have a relationship with my wonderful mother.

I have a relationship with my siblings.

I have a relationship with the guys I play basketball with as well as guys I work out with.

I have relationships with my church family.

I have relationships with my business partners.

I have relationships even with the ones that have passed away. How? Because I remember the time that I shared with them.

Value your relationships. The reality is that you need all of them to make you who you are.

**TAKEAWAY:** Life is short. Enjoy it and the relationships it brings.

#OGHBYRG

## DAY 88:
## WHAT GOT YOU HERE – WON'T GET YOU ANY FURTHER.

*"So many people are losing value each year, declining in earning ability, because they are not continually upgrading their knowledge and skills."* – Brian Tracy

Listen family, whatever knowledge or skill set you have is being replaced quickly. If not today, it will be tomorrow. If you're not upgrading in your craft or business and your competitors are, guess what? You lose! It's that simple. Step your game up. What got you where you are will definitely keep you where you are.

Do more, be more, live more!

**TAKEAWAY:** Be grateful for where you are and get excited for where you're headed.

#OGHBYRG

# DAY 89: CONFIDENCE!

We all make mistakes and we all come up short at some point in life. The difference between a successful person and someone who is not successful has a lot to do with confidence.

The successful person learns from the mistake and gains confidence, but the unsuccessful person loses confidence never to try again.

Confidence comes after you commit; take courage and realize that you are capable.

Do me and yourself a huge favor. Go right back to the thing that you couldn't do and get it done!

You need a push?

Your team needs structure?

Your department needs a plan of action?

You need help in reaching your goals?

Contact me and let my team and I help you.

**TAKEAWAY:** *"If you don't have confidence you will always find a way not to win."* – Carl Lewis

#OGHBYRG

# DAY 90: HOW BAD DO YOU WANT IT?

I am not just talking about on the surface level.

I know that this is day 90. I know that you've worked so hard and have come so far, but this is not a 90-day program. Nope, this is not a 3-month fix. This is your life!

When you first opened this book, you made a promise to commit! You signed up for 365 days, so don't get satisfied with where you are.

Yes, you've lost weight.

Yes, you got your sexy back.

Yes, you're more disciplined.

Yes, people have noticed your better you.

We don't do better we do best!

Congrats on 90 days but we have so much work to do. Picture yourself on day 365. Can you only imagine what they'll say about you then? I can. See you tomorrow.

**TAKEAWAY:** Don't try to do a year's work in 90 days because you can't.

#OGHBYRG

## DAY 91: YOU'RE AMAZING!

My daughters did a tribute dance to their mom for her birthday. They danced to a song called "You're Amazing," by Ricky Dillard. They wanted to do this because they have an amazing mom!

Guess what? You're pretty amazing as well! You must tell yourself sometimes that you are, as well as pat yourself on the back.

This doesn't mean you're stuck up or arrogant. It simply means that you see the strides that you've made to become better and you are better! Not only are you better but everything attached to you is better.

So, rock on with your bad self! You're amazing!

**TAKEAWAY:** Go give someone your autograph now, because you're about to blow up!

#OGHBYRG

## DAY 92: MAKE A DECISION!

These 3 words are so powerful but must be done and not just said.

You have so much more to accomplish but you need to make the decision! It could be the decision to change careers because you've lost the desire for what you do currently.

It could be making the decision to change your eating habits. It could be the decision to change your circle of friends.

Whatever it may be stop procrastinating and make the decision!

You have to make a decision that you're going to pay the price and go the distance in order to achieve the goals you have set for yourself.

What's holding you back?

Make a decision!

**TAKEAWAY:** Be apart of the 20 percent that lead or the 80 percent that follow. It's all in your decision.

#OGHBYRG

## DAY 93: BE THE LEADER YOU NEVER HAD.

It's easy to blame an outside factor on what goes wrong in our lives. We say, *"If this hadn't happened or I had someone to guide me, I'd be better off."*

Well family, the reality is that it did happen.

They did walk out on you.

They did mistreat you on purpose.

You didn't have what others had growing up!

What you do have is that comeback! That's right... Every time you get knocked down or counted out, you always comeback!

So, I am challenging you today to pick yourself up, stop having a pity party, and get back.

Be the leader you never had! You can do this!

Find a mentor or a life coach to help you through this process. You know where you are now get help to where you want to be.

**TAKEAWAY:** *"Everything I wanted in my life, I try to be in someone else's."* – Marlon Lock

#OGHBYRG

## DAY 94:
## FAITH WILL TAKE YOU HIGHER THAN YOU EVER IMAGINED!

Whatever your destination is, faith can get you there.

Step out and activate your faith. Go places you've only dreamed of. Step out:

In your walk with God

In your marriage

In your family

In your business

In your finances

In your healing

On all levels!

Remember: You got me pushing you the entire way.

**TAKEAWAY:** You will reach above and beyond your imagination if you just have faith!

#OGHBYRG

## DAY 95:
## IT'S OUR ANNIVERSARY.

Okay where do I begin?

Some years ago, in 2002 God did one of the most amazing things in my life. He blessed me with my wife.

He knew where I was headed, so He just literally gave me who could help me along the way.

Do we have issues? Ummmm yeah, I am sure all marriages do (even the ones who pretend like they don't... but that ain't none of my business). I honestly must admit that this one right here – my wife – was only responsible 5% of the time. So that leaves me with the other 95%. I just want to let everyone know to truly value and appreciate what you do have.

I can't imagine life without my wife by my side. Truly a God-send! She keeps me balanced and at ease and I keep her going.

To my wife, the years have gone by extremely fast. We've lost some pretty amazing people and we've gained some as well, and you've been there all the time.

I left the police force and you had my back.

I became an assistant pastor and you had my back.

I became a senior pastor and you had my back.

I wanted a music career and you had my back.

You took my daughter in as if you had her (that was huge) and had her back.

Having done all of this and so much more, since I can speak life and death, these next years together will be more than you've ever imagined. I got you!

**TAKEAWAY:** Anniversaries of any kind should be applauded and celebrated!

#OGHBYRG

## DAY 96: YOU STILL GOT TIME!

What's the problem? Why are you still in the same place, with the same problems and the same mind set you had at the beginning of the year?

Don't you want better? Don't you think you deserve better? Well I am here to let you know that you do!

You got goals that you still can reach.

You got weight you still can lose.

You got a book you still can write.

You got a deal you still can close.

You got a marriage you still can fix.

You got a child you still can help.

You got a room you still can makeover.

You got some prayers still not answered.

You got some calls you still can make.

Please do it now, while you still got time!

**TAKEAWAY:** The fact that you woke up this morning means that you still got time.

#OGHBYRG

# DAY 97: NOTHING LIKE A MOTHER.

If I tried to put in words how much my mother means to me, I'd run out of room.

When I think of my mom, I get a sensation that runs through my body and it makes me proud. Why?

My mother is the strongest woman that I know.

At age 11, I lost my dad to a drug overdose and my mother stepped up like a champ and gave me and my brothers the best life possible! We didn't get everything we wanted but she definitely gave us everything that we needed! I saw my mother day in and day out sacrifice to make our lives incredible! I saw my mother go without so that we could have. I saw my mother go hungry so that my brothers and I could eat.

My mom made struggling fun!

If you have your mother or a mother-like figure in your life, love and spoil her everyday of her life.

If you're not on one accord with your mom, fix it because once she's gone, she's gone. To my mom, I love you a whole bunch and thank you for loving me unconditionally.

**TAKEAWAY:** There's nothing in the world like a mother.

#OGHBYRG

# DAY 98: WILL YOU BE READY?

There is an opportunity that's going to present itself to you. The question is, will you be ready?

It's so easy to think that you're preparing when actually you're just waiting.

Waiting is passively sitting back hoping an opportunity comes up.

Preparing is aggressively going after what you know is yours.

I'd rather be prepared and not have the opportunity than to have the opportunity and not be prepared.

Make sure that you're ready when opportunity knocks. When it knocks you be the one to open the door.

In my life so many times I was ready and looked at it as a disappointment when I wasn't picked or selected. Then, when I realized that the disappointments were based on my work ethic, I changed. My work ethic paid off and one day one door opened for me that was the gateway to every other door. Keep at it. You are closer than you think.

**TAKEAWAY:** Don't ever have to get ready, stay ready!

#OGHBYRG

## DAY 99:
## THERE IS NOTHING MORE POWERFUL THAN A CHANGED MIND.

I must give you your medicine for today.

I need you to get up from where you are and get to where you're suppose to be!

You've been stuck in the same place all because you haven't changed your mind. There is nothing in the world more powerful than a changed mind.

A changed mind will take you from good to great!

A changed mind will take you from not enough to more than enough!

Don't change your outfit.

Don't change your hair style.

Don't change jobs.

Don't change churches.

Don't change cities.

Change your mind!!

**TAKEAWAY:** Change the thoughts you think about you everyday, and your life will change.

#OGHBYRG

## DAY 100: MY INSPIRATION

Wow wow wow!!! This has truly been incredible for me to be able to motivate, inspire and encourage you these past 99 days in a row, and here we are at 100 days!

As much as I hear how I've inspired people, please know that you, the people, are the ones that inspire me. My life used to be a mess. While I felt that I looked pretty good on the outside, inside I was struggling. It was to the point that I considered taking my own life. But to look back at what God did for me, truly makes me go the extra mile for others.

I am not telling you what to believe in or who to believe in. What I am telling you is that Jesus Christ changed my life completely and if He'll do it for me, I can't wait to see what He's going to do for you.

If you know Jesus as your savior, please share this with someone that doesn't. Someone is waiting on you.

If you think these last 100 days were something, wait until these next 100.

Thanks for trusting me to take you on this journey these first 100 days. I am not tired yet and I hope that you are not as well. See you tomorrow.

**TAKEAWAY:** Go celebrate! Look how far you've come and how well you are doing! Rock on with yo' bad self.

#OGHBYRG

## DAY 101: SHOOT THE SHOT!

These next 100 days will be incredible!

I am gonna push you to levels you've only dreamed of, and help you get to places in life that seemed impossible.

Yes, you! With all the mess ups, mistakes, doors closed in your face, yes with all of that, you are still going to get it!

I've learned that all anyone needs is a little encouragement and some people to push them!

There is one requirement I ask of you. I need you to shoot the shot! Yes, I need you to go for it.

If not now, when? You deserve to reach your goals. Think about once you get what you desire, and all the lives you can change for the better. I know that's what you want, so I am telling you to go get it!

**TAKEAWAY:** Everyone misses, but what about when you make it.

#OGHBYRG

## DAY 102: BE OF GOOD COURAGE AND HAVE NO FEAR.

Our past mistakes can truly keep us from moving forward.

What if you succeed? Yeah that's right, what if everything turns out well? Don't be afraid. I need you to go for it! I am in your life for a reason, let me help you.

You got this! Tell fear: *"It was nice meeting you because you taught me things about myself that I needed to know, but now it's time to say goodbye."*

**TAKEAWAY:** *"Courage is not absence of fear, it is control of fear."* – Mark Twain

#OGHBYRG

## DAY 103: GET IT DONE!!

Today I am tired, and don't feel like working out. I don't feel like going to work. I don't feel like going to school. I don't feel like smiling. I don't feel like going to church. I don't feel like going the first mile so how can I do two? But you know what?

I realize that I made a commitment to myself, and I have to draw strength from the core of who I am and who I believe in. Time for beast mode! Since nobody will give it to me... I'll get it myself.

Same rules apply for you, so get it done!

**TAKEAWAY:** No matter if it is a little or if it is much, get it done.

#OGHBYRG

## DAY 104: SLAY THE DRAGON OF HABIT!

To get something you've never had, you must do something you've never done.

I am challenging you to break your habits. Yes! Your habits. Obviously if you're doing something that's working, by all means keep doing it; but if you are still frustrated, never satisfied, and you're still with the same people doing the same old crazy stuff and being left with the same crazy results... well you might want to change.

Let's refocus and rid ourselves of the foolishness and change our habits today!

Do something inspiring. Do something with your family, like read a book, play Uno, or just talk.

I need you to slay that dragon! Love y'all family and there's nothing that you can do about it.

**TAKEAWAY:** Once I slayed my dragon of bad habits, I was left with good habits.

#OGHBYRG

## DAY 105: THERE'S NOTHING LIKE A CHANGED MIND!

Hey family, I need you all to get this if you don't get anything else. If you're willing to change how you think, you can change your entire life. There's nothing more powerful than a changed mind.

It's time out for talking about change and it's time to really change!

It may seem hard.

It may be difficult.

You will lose some loved ones who you thought were close to you, but just know it'll all be worth it in the long run.

Now let's get it family and make that change.

**TAKEAWAY:** *"If I can change and you can change then everybody can change."* – Rocky Balboa

#OGHBYRG

## DAY 106 & 107: AS THE CHALLENGE ESCALATES, THE NEED FOR TEAMWORK ELEVATES!

This is known as The Law of Mount Everest. – John Maxwell.

All it means is that the more difficult the challenge, the more you must work as a team. Working as a team is not always the easiest thing to do.

When you become a part of a team, then the individual you has to die so that the team can live!

The reason this can be challenging is because most people feel that they are right. That is not a negative thing. All of your life you've made choices based on how you felt. Whether right or wrong you had to deal with that choice; however, as a team, you must look at all sides and factors that play a role in the team's success.

There are some levels that you're going to reach but you can't reach them without the proper team and teamwork.

There are some goals that you are going to crush still this year, but it's going to take teamwork!

Please pay close attention! If you have any of these on your team get rid of them today:

Jealousy

Backstabbers

Busy bodies

Laziness

Average

Does just enough

Late

Doubters

These are only a few team-breaking issues. It is okay to relieve those team members who display these types of behaviors. We do not have time to waste to get to our purpose. Love them but find somewhere else they can be used, if they choose to stick around. Trust me, it'll save you time, money and headaches in the end.

**TAKEAWAY:** *"You are the sum of the five people you associate with the most."* – John Maxwell

#OGHBYRG

## DAY 108: WATCH OUT FOR "I AM JUST PLAYING."

This is a rough one today but it's going to help somebody.

In route to your destiny, there will be people that will say things to knock you down, get you off track, and truly frustrate you, but then they'll say, *"oh I am just playing"* or, *"why you take stuff so serious?"*

Please don't fall for that!

First of all, they are not just playing, they truly mean it. Their reply was based upon the reaction of you and those who may have been around. Secondarily, life is serious. What you are passionate about is serious. What you've gone to school for to increase in knowledge and your overall value is serious. The 5 pounds you lost is serious - before you can lose 50 pounds you have to lose 5 pounds first.

Love y'all family and ain't nothing you can do about it!

**TAKEAWAY:** A guy once told me that he doesn't play. That's why he left school early because they had recess. Life is not a game so stop playing.

#OGHBYRG

## DAY 109: YOU'VE COME TOO FAR TO GIVE UP NOW.

Drake said, *"Before you give up, think about why you hung on for so long."*

I can relate to feelings of being frustrated and moments that you may want to throw in the towel, but I can't let you do that. You've come too far to turn back now. Think of why you started in the first place.

Remember this 365-day journey was all about you. You became intentional, you saw the value in yourself, so you started adding value to yourself and you've been consistent for the most part.

Remember:

If it doesn't challenge you...

If it doesn't make you dream about it...

If it doesn't frustrate you until it's right...

If it doesn't make you cry and laugh...

If it doesn't push you to the limit...

Do you really want it?

Yeah you do, that's why you grind so hard everyday. Keep

grinding and I'll see you somewhere at the top. When you see me, just shout out *"OGHBYRG!"* (pronounced AWG-BERG)

**TAKEAWAY:** *"Before you quit think about why you started."* – 21Day Fix

#OGHBYRG

## DAY 110: MIRACLES HAPPEN EVERYDAY!

Yes, that's right, miracles happen everyday.

You don't hear about them everyday or you may not recognize them, but they do happen. You are a miracle that happened today because you are reading this. The fact that you woke up and someone else didn't today, makes you a miracle.

What if today was the day that your entire situation turned around for the better?

What if today was the day that someone gave you another chance?

What if today was the day that the pain you've been dealing with in your body left?

Please know that this happens everyday. Doctors can't explain it, family members don't understand it, and friends can't believe it but happens.

Here is what you need to do: Get into position for your miracle. Prepare for it now and when it shows up you are ready for it.

**TAKEAWAY:** *"If I fail to prepare then I am preparing to fail."*

#OGHBYRG

## DAY 111: DOWN BUT NOT OUT!

In life you must make proper and timely adjustments. When one area is at a stand still, work on another area. It's always something that you can work on and get better at.

Just know, because you're down in one area you're not out in another one.

**TAKEAWAY:** Your ability to adjust will be your ability to win.

#OGHBYRG

## DAY 112: YOU'VE GOT WHAT IT TAKES!

As you can tell from the past 111 days, I am not going to ever stop believing in you.

Every relationship I've been in I've never left the person, they always leave me. Now I've had to take the blame but no worries, God knows. So just know you can't get rid of me!

I don't care what the situation is, what you may be dealing with right now, you're going to get through it! You want to know why? You got through the last situation, and you're going to get through this situation because you got what it takes.

**TAKEAWAY:** *"Sometimes the teacher, sometimes the student, but always a friend."* – Greg Francis

#OGHBYRG

## DAY 113: MAKE THE ADJUSTMENT!

Maybe you made a resolution at the beginning of the year and you haven't followed through with it.

We've all made this mistake at some point in some area. I need you to make the proper adjustment. What is the proper adjustment? Let me help you.

If what you're doing right now is hurting you, causing you frustration and it's not connected with your vision and you cry more than smile... adjust! We spend too much time stuck in the same miserable place when all we have to do is adjust. Do what you have to do now, so that you can do what you want to do later.

**TAKEAWAY:** When we lay down at night and our initial position becomes uncomfortable, what do we do? We simply adjust.

#OGHBYRG

## DAY 114: DEVELOP A GREAT REPUTATION!

Brian Tracy says, *"There is nothing that will bring you more quickly to the attention of people who can help you than for you to develop a reputation for hard, disciplined work, every hour of every day."*

You should want your reputation to be so incredible that even the ones that don't *"care for you,"* will vouch for you.

Start today, start now and change your reputation. If you already have a good one, keep it. One mistake can affect all the great things you've done. Stay focused.

Love y'all family.

**TAKEAWAY:** *"A good name is far better than a lot of money son."* – Elbridge Lock (granddad)

#OGHBYRG

## DAY 115:
## IF YOU "LIVE" FOR THE COMPLIMENT, THEN YOU'LL "DIE" FROM THE CRITICISM.

Hey family I am a firm believer in whatever I do, do it so God is pleased.

If God is pleased, then everything else will fall into place.

We must be careful that we don't live for the *"likes."* What's the likes? It's the hearts you get on Instagram and the follows you get on Facebook. Social media can be a great asset if used the right way, but it can be a headache if used wrong and for the wrong reasons.

We get so caught up in everyone else liking us that when they don't like us, we tend to not like ourselves. The same mouth that compliments you is the same mouth that will scandalize your name.

Take the compliment, be polite and say, "thank you."

**TAKEAWAY:** *"Be your biggest fan as well as your worse critic."* – Marlon Lock

#OGHBYRG

# DAY 116: BE PROACTIVE INSTEAD OF REACTIVE.

First off, I am gonna start off by letting you know that this was tough for me in the beginning. I was the type of person where it was easy for me to take life as it happened. My favorite line was, *"God is in control."* The reality is that God gave me the ability to control what He was in control of.

Yes, God is in control, but He gives us all choice. The choice to be proactive and stay ahead of the game is totally up to each of us as individuals.

Let's not wait too late and miss out on the opportunity that's about to present itself. Don't *"get ready,"* always *"stay ready!"* Get it done so when the door opens, you're qualified to walk through it.

**TAKEAWAY:** I read in the Bible, in the book of Deuteronomy 30:19 and it changed my life. Now you read it.

#OGHBYRG

## DAY 117: THE SECRET SURVEY.

Imagine that on Monday your job is bringing in an undercover agent to find out who they can promote for this big-time position! I mean you will go from what you make now to an additional $100,000 a year. The company won't tell you this, but these secret spies will be watching your every move.

Are you punctual?

How well do you get along with co-workers?

Do you create a great work environment?

Do you exceed expectations or just meet them?

How's your energy and focus?

Are you respected?

Do you promote gossip, or do you kill it?

Factors like these play a critical role in the success of any business or relationship. Either you're giving your best effort or your worst effort. If you're going to do anything, why not give your all?

Know this: It is not a secret. Everyone knows who the lazy person is!

Everyone knows who takes short cuts!

Everyone knows who's always late and always leaves early. Make a choice to be the best that you can be all the time.

**TAKEAWAY:** If you are not going to go hard then please don't go at all.

#OGHBYRG

## DAY 118: YOU'RE STRONGER THAN THE STORM!

There are so many storms; from hail storms to sand storms and wind storms.

Then there are life storms. Oh yes, this storm right here can take you out in so many ways and on so many levels. How do we prepare for life storms? By sitting down and seeing where you are and where you want to be. Then, put together a plan to get there.

For me, I always pray first and ask God to help me and whatever lesson I need to get out of the storm I can receive it! Looking at the storm as an opportunity to learn makes the storm so much easier to deal with.

I know life can bring so many things your way, and what's crazy is that it can come all at the same time. Let me encourage you today. You are stronger than your storm!

**TAKEAWAY:** The next time you are in a storm, chase it! Your rainbow is just on the other side.

#OGHBYRG

## DAY 119:
## BE A STORM CHASER.

The world meteorological organization every year give names to the hurricanes of that particular year, but they forgot the name of the one who can calm the storm. Jesus!

*"Then he arose and rebuked the wind, and said to the sea, "peace, be still!" And the wind ceased and there was a great calm."* Mark 4:39 NKJV

I know from personal experience that with Jesus on your side you can be a storm chaser!

**TAKEAWAY:** Tell somebody I am stronger than the storm!

#OGHBYRG

## DAY 120: PAY THE PRICE.

It's easy to want better but the question becomes what are you doing to get better? You must be willing to pay the price.

Here is a scenario. If you want to go higher in your field do these 3 things everyday.

1. Get to work earlier than anyone else.

2. Work hard (give your best effort) while at work.

3. Stay later than anyone else.

Trust me you will get noticed!

We often want what others have but we're not willing to pay the price they've paid. Pay the price now to change the course of your future. Keep in mind it's more than just you depending on you.

**TAKEAWAY:** People usually just see the reward you get publicly but have no idea what you did privately.

#OGHBYRG

# DAY 121: SUPPORT FAMILY.

My little cousin had a basketball game today. I told my kids and they started screaming, *"Can we go to the game, can we go to the game?"*

I'll admit, my family that I grew up with is not nearly as close as we should be. It's sad but it's also reality.

Take the time to support family. Not foolishness, but family. Sometimes family are not the ones you have a blood relationship with. Recognize what it means to have a family and support them.

**TAKEAWAY:** *"Success always takes help."* – Simon Sinek

#OGHBYRG

## DAY 122: ENJOY THE SIMPLE THINGS IN LIFE.

I get home from an awesome workout only to find my mother outside grilling.

I've lost so many close people in my life. At my age, now I view life differently. I pray my mom lives to be a healthy 100 years old but it's in God's hands.

The reality is, I must enjoy the special people and moments in my life while I can, for as long as I can. I have a very, very small circle of friends and people I trust. But I have a huge community of people that I love and rock with.

I value each friendship and relationship, regardless of the status. I work hard! I play hard! I love hard! I want God to get the glory out of everything that I do!

Enjoy the simple things in life like a meal, a conversation, a walk, a hug, a kiss, a text, because you never know when that'll be the last one.

Love y'all family and ain't nothing you can do about it.

**TAKEAWAY:** Here today, gone tomorrow, so true.

#OGHBYRG

## DAY 123: WE CAN FAIL ALONE.

Please pay close attention to today's message. I really need you to get this and get it fast. This is day 123 and you have come so far! I am so proud of you but don't think for one second you got here by yourself.

There is no way that I made it to where I am by myself and there is no way I would allow my mind to make me think that. That is totally false information!

I told you a few days ago that success always takes help. Success in any area in life takes help but failure you can do all by yourself.

Get with people that motivate you to be better then do better and live better! Have a circle of people that if you fall, they are right there picking you back up supporting you!

**TAKEAWAY:** *"Yes, you can fail alone, but you don't have to fail at all."* – Marlon Lock

#OGHBYRG

## DAY 124: WHO YOU CALLING SILLY?

In 2012, my wife wrote her first book called, Who You Calling Silly? How a Silly Woman Becomes Virtuous. This book is awesome and has helped so many people.

Initially, most thought that it was a book to empower women (and it truly does), but what I noticed was that so many men were reading the book as well. The subtitle is, "How a silly woman becomes virtuous."

The book basically shows how we all at some point in our lives have made silly mistakes or intentional silly choices. If not careful, we can stay in those choices that we made way longer then we need to.

Then the book shows step-by-step how to become virtuous and use your silly moments as mastery moments. What's a mastery moment? I like to call it those moments that were there to break you, but they made you!

Yeah that's right, mastery moments cause you to go from tragedy to triumph! From not enough to more than enough!

Don't let anyone call you silly based on your past. Simply look at them and say, *"Who you callin' silly?"*

**TAKEAWAY:** You can always turn your situation around.

#OGHBYRG

## DAY 125: RANDOM ACT OF KINDNESS

Do something nice for someone just because. Don't have a hidden agenda or an ulterior motive, just do it! Don't expect anything in return and watch how freaking awesome you feel!

Here are some examples:

Go to a Starbucks and pay for the car behind you in line.

Go to a homeless shelter and drop off a bunch of hats, gloves and scarves.

Order pizza for your department for lunch just because.

Send your significant other some pretty flowers.

Here's one more. Tell God thank you.

Now get up and go do it.

**TAKEAWAY:** What you do for others will be done to you.

#OGHBYRG

## DAY 126: GO FOR IT.

So many of us dread Mondays. When we had all the weekend to relax, spend time with family, get revived from an awesome church service, sleep in longer, etc. It's so easy to get into a negative mind-set about the upcoming work week. You have no energy, no drive, no excitement, but let me help you.

This week, I want you to go for it! I mean be the best that you can be.

There is nobody better fit, better equipped, for the task at hand.

You got nothing to lose but everything to gain! Your job assignment is not for *"the company you work for,"* it's for all those depending on you to work! You've got somebody depending on you that matters.

**TAKEAWAY:** Go for it today. What if it works?

#OGHBYRG

# DAY 127:
# DEALING WITH CONFLICT

Conflict is something that we all must deal with at some point whether we want to or not, right?

The problem really isn't the conflict, it's how we respond to it.

Here's a few tips I want to share, and I pray they work for you as they have for me.

1. Maintain a quiet spirit.

2. View the conflict as coming from the Lord

- don't be angry

- don't be critical

- don't be upset

- - don't be bitter

3. Ask the person is there anything that you could've done to make the situation better, receive their response and then simply say "thank you."

I am not saying this is easy, but I am saying to at least give it a try.

Thank you, Dr. Charles Stanley for teaching me this. You will never know the impact it has had on my life. Just know

I am forever grateful.

**TAKEAWAY:** My Grandma Lock would always say, "When you know better, do better." She's saying it to you now.

#OGHBYRG

## DAY 128: CHECK ON SOMEONE YOU HAVEN'T CHECKED ON IN A WHILE.

Thanks to my baby girl (Evangelist Sydney) for inspiring me today.

Often with the busy-ness of life, we forget to check on others. I don't think it's done intentionally to be rude or unconcerned, it's just that life kind of gets in the way. My Sydney is the most thoughtful girl on planet earth. She's so caring and considerate and always asks me about people or family we may haven't seen or talked to in a while.

It can be a text, email, letter, or how about picking up the phone and giving them a call. You'd be surprised how much this would mean to someone.

Go ahead and make the call, send that text.

**TAKEAWAY:** It's the little things that truly mean so much. Thank you, Syd, for always keeping me on point. Daddy loves you.

#OGHBYRG

## DAY 129: WHO ARE YOU?

Jim Rohn says, *"You are an average of the 5 people you spend most of your time with."*

Wow! This statement says a lot. Real quick, write down the 5 people that you are around or associate with the most.

Now look at each one of those names and write down the good they bring out of you and then the not so good (be honest and it may hurt).

Hopefully the pros outweighed the cons. If you need to get you a new *"fav 5"* then do it immediately! Your future depends on it.

It's important family that you spend time with the right people; positive people with good energy

and good vibes.

Whatever I am a part of, I want it to be festive and alive!

**TAKEAWAY:** Whatever shows up "dead..." I bury it! If you don't bury it, it will bury you.

#OGHBYRG

# DAY 130: HAVE SOME FUN!

Life is short, go have some fun.

Pay attention. I didn't say go out and do the wrong things, I said have some fun. When people hang out with me or get a chance to see me in a different light other than behind the pulpit, I often get the response or reaction of, *"Man I can't believe we had that much fun and didn't drink any alcohol, we didn't mess around with any women, we didn't do the wrong things and we had an incredible time."* I then ask the question, *"Is drinking until I pass out fun? Is messing around with a woman that's not my wife and breaking up my home and family and losing the trust of my wife and children fun? Is being confrontational and getting into it with others while I am out fun?"*

If that is the definition of fun, then I'd rather not have any. The reality is that it's not fun. It's frustrating and stressful!

**TAKEAWAY:** If your idea of fun is affecting you in a negative way, is it really fun?

#OGHBYRG

# DAY 131: CARE ABOUT YOUR COMMUNITY.

Each year we hear about communities that thrive and are pleasant places to live in. We also hear about communities that are failing. What's interesting is that these communities are not far at all from one another.

What's the difference? I'll tell you. One community cares and the other community doesn't.

I've heard some say that society or the government does not care about certain areas. While this may be true, do you really care?

Here's a way to find out if you care.

Do you do community clean ups in your area?

- If not don't talk about it being dirty

Do you promote neighborhood block watch in your area?

- If not don't talk about the crime rate

Do you cut your grass and shovel your sidewalks regularly and maintain a nice well-kept area?

- If not then don't complain about what the city is doing

I've learned in my life that most people complain about what they are not doing. Please don't be that person.

**TAKEAWAY:** Write out some things that you want to see done in your community to better it and reach out to your alderman, your mayor, or your chief of police and make it happen. That's your right.

Remember it always starts with one.

#OGHBYRG

## DAY 132:
## GET OUT OF THE WAY.

It is so easy to get in our own way. We allow things such as doubt, frustration, fear, or even past mistakes to hinder us from progressing and moving forward. LISTEN! It. Is. Over!

Do not allow the enemy of self to make you think you cannot do it (whatever it may be to you).

**TAKEAWAY:** Tell yourself, "Move. Get out the way."

#OGHBYRG

## DAY 133: CONTRIBUTE

Make sure you do your part today and then help someone else with theirs.

Don't ever be the person that just shows up with nothing in your hand, even if you were told not to bring anything. Contribute.

Contribute to the party snacks at the office.

Contribute to your church's clothing drive.

Contribute for thanksgiving dinner (host it at your house for Pete's sake).

Contribute to doing the laundry.

Contribute on gas money.

Contribute with washing dishes.

I think you get the point.

John Maxwell said, *"We live in a culture that awards people trophies for simply showing up, regardless of their contributions."* Don't let that be you. Contribute.

**TAKEAWAY:** I used the term, *"for Pete's sake."* Does anyone know who Pete is? Well, forget Pete, do it for your sake. You would want someone to do the same for you.

#OGHBYRG

## DAY 134: YOU ARE NOT ALONE.

Ok, it's crunch time and everyone you've been depending on seems to have left you or let you down.

Those that you've helped won't seem to help you. I know you may feel alone but the reality is that we all feel alone at times. Some of the most famous and successful people on paper that get all the attention in the crowded room, still feel alone.

I got some good news for you, you are not alone! I need you to say it out loud, so you can hear yourself say it. Say, *"I am not alone!"*

The enemy loves isolation. If he can get you alone then you'll be vulnerable. You'll have thoughts like *"nobody loves me"* or *"no ones checked on me"* or *"I am not good enough."*

Stop listening to what wants to bring you down and hear the voice that's lifting you up!

**TAKEAWAY:** Life can be crazy and frustrating but just know that you are not alone. Now go crush some dreams today!

#OGHBYRG

## DAY 135: BE HUMBLE.

You crushed some dreams on yesterday and made it through your feelings of loneliness so congratulations!

You have so many more things that you'll accomplish this year, which is setting you up for the best new life ever! Man, I can't wait to see you this time next year! As a matter of fact, give yourself your own autograph because you're about to blow up!

I need you to do me a small favor that will bring huge results, though. I need you to stay humble. I know you want to gloat in your critics' faces and hit your chest, because they doubted you and counted you out, but you have way too much class for that. By doing that you make them feel like they matter.

**TAKEAWAY:** The best way to silence dream killers is to be successful.

#OGHBYRG

## DAY 136: THERE'S A TIME AND SEASON FOR EVERYTHING!

I know how difficult it can be to be so close and want something so bad and you exhaust all your energy and efforts with all the right intentions, and it still seems to come up short!

I know what it is to have loved ones depending on you to make it happen and the reality is you can't.

You must keep in mind that there's a time and a season for everyone and everything. What if you wanted something so bad that you got it but weren't ready to handle it? What would happen? You would lose it all and have to start all over again.

Take this season of *"pause"* in your life. That's right, pause. Just at the right time God is going to push the "play" button.

You are much closer than you think! It's not that what you're doing isn't working, it's just not the time! Know that your efforts and energy are not in vain!

Get ready because your season is approaching fast! You got me with you all the way!

**TAKEAWAY:** Read Ecclesiastes 3:1; Denzel Washington

says, *"When you pray for rain you have to deal with the mud too."*

#OGHBYRG

# DAY 137: WHOSE REPORT WILL YOU BELIEVE?

The enemy wants you to believe lies, but God wants you to believe the truth!

What's the truth? Jesus saves, and God loves you.

Now you might be a skeptic and don't believe like I believe and that's fine. I am not here to make you be who I think you should be, but I will tell you that who and what I believe in is a pretty sweet deal. Check this out:

I was able to take all my issues (all of them), give them to the Lord and He gave me a clean slate! Are you kidding me? I just want you to believe in something more than the problems that you keep having. You don't have to believe the negative report when a better one is one step away.

**TAKEAWAY:** Now who's report will you believe?

#OGHBYRG

# DAY 138: A BETTER WAY.

You may know me as a pastor, motivator, a life coach, a musician, singer or songwriter; and all those are pretty cool. I enjoy each one of them.

You may know me as a husband and a dad. Trust me, I would not trade these for anything in the world. My wife and children mean everything to me and there is nothing that I wouldn't do for them (legally that is).

I would like to share with you who I really am. I am a child of God. I was called to preach at the age of 5 and preached my first sermon at age 10. My subject was *"God is a good God."* I came from the scripture St. John 3:16 (pretty cool right for a 10-year-old).

I never knew how my life would be or where I would end up or what I'd be doing. I always knew that it would involve helping people because I've loved helping people since a child.

Today I just want to offer someone a better way.

Not more money. Not more friends. Not a better house or car, but truly a better way.

What's that way you ask? For me it was giving my life to Christ, and after I strayed away (yes, I strayed) I rededicated my life back to Him. If life seems all out of control and if you feel that you have done everything right, but everything still seems wrong, try Jesus. Try a better way.

**TAKEAWAY:** To anyone who may not be believer in Jesus Christ, this was not meant to be offensive, but I must be who God has chosen me to be and I am not ashamed of the gospel of Jesus Christ. It is because of Him and Him only that I move and have my being. So just turn the page. See you in day 139.

#OGHBYRG

## DAY 139: KEEP A LEVELED HEAD.

I was at an airport on the escalator headed to baggage claim and the escalator was going down. I immediately thought about life and how we often plan and prepare for going up but have no strategy for coming down.

Therefore, having a leveled head is so critical to having a healthy balance in life.

**TAKEAWAY:** "Never get too high. You must come down. Never get too low that you feel you can't come up." – Marlon Lock

#OGHBYRG

## DAY 140:
## WORK HARD AND WAIT HARD.

Nobody truly likes to wait, I think that's fair for me to say. Just look at society:

We like the drive-through restaurant service.

We order movie tickets in advance, online.

We do express check out.

We honk the horn as soon as a light turns green.

We shop online.

We are truly a microwave society, but please don't let the pace of society cause you to be in such a hurry that you move too fast.

Some things really do take time. For example:

Relationships

Marriages

Raising a family

Goals

Don't become impatient. I know you are working hard and continue to do so, but I also need you to wait even more. Your breakthrough is on the way, just wait!

**TAKEAWAY:** Psalms 40:1 says, *"I waited patiently for the*

*Lord; and he inclined unto me and heard my cry."*

#OGHBYRG

## DAY 141: BEHAVIOR IS THE ONLY TRUTH.

Winston Churchill says, *"I long ago stopped listening to what people say, instead I look at what they do. Behavior is the only truth."*

This statement was made many years ago but it's just as true today as it was back then. Please know that you will be known by your actions not by your speech.

We have seen throughout history where presidential candidates make all the promises in the world to get in office but do nothing they said once they get the seat.

Remember this: Actions truly speak louder than words.

Be a doer and not just a talker. Get it done! You can do it!

**TAKEAWAY:** *"When someone shows you who they are, believe them."* – Michael Lock

#OGHBYRG

# DAY 142: LIFE IS NOT A DRESS REHEARSAL.

Family, if you have never listened to me before and even if you don't plan to in the future, I need you to hear and do this: Take control of your life!

For me, that was giving my life to God. I had to let God know that I was in a bad place and could not get out of it without His help. I told God that I was sorry, I then asked for His forgiveness in Jesus's name and guess what? My life changed immediately for the better!

Did I still have issues? Yes.

Did I still get frustrated? Yes.

Were doors still closed in my face? Yes.

With God I have a sense of peace that makes all my difficult situations easier to deal with. That works this day for me.

I got to a point in my life where it was no longer a game, life was real, and I had no plans and it showed! Maybe you or someone you know is at a super low point in life with no direction. Get them a copy of this book immediately. It's been helping you, I know it will help them.

**TAKEAWAY:** Life is not a dress rehearsal. It's the real

thing, and it is happening right now!

#OGHBYRG

# DAY 143: LEAD ME AS I LEAD YOUR PEOPLE.

Life happens suddenly. Before you recognize it, you are in a position that you did not even know you were qualified for. Do not worry; do not fear. You are right where you are supposed to be! If God brought you to it – He will bring you through it!

Just make sure that you acknowledge God in everything that you do, so that He can provide clear direction. Be the best leader you can always be because someone is following you.

Daily, I ask God to lead me as I lead others.

**TAKEAWAY:** One cannot truly lead others if unable to lead himself or herself.

#OGHBYRG

## DAY 144: EVERY CHILD DESERVES TO BE A CHILD.

I pray your week has been awesome and your weekend will be even better.

I really want to speak to you today from a special place in my heart, regarding children. You know there is not a child born that had a chance to pick their parents, siblings, or environment. A child is just born into the world.

I want you to understand that a child never asked to be here, they just know that they're here and they hope for the best.

We as adults must make sure that we allow our kids to be kids. All they want is love and affection and to know that you care. If you have children, young or old, please reach out to them and let them know that you love them.

To my oldest baby girl Tone'y, I love you a whole bunch. Although you are the oldest of your siblings you will always be my "baby girl" – love dad.

**TAKEAWAY:** My granddad told me that a parent should always want their children to have a better life than they did. I agree.

#OGHBYRG

## DAY 145: JUST BELIEVE!

I need you to believe in yourself right at this very moment!

Believe that you are the best.

Believe that you can do it.

Believe that you can make it.

Believe that it's yours.

Believe you're destined for greatness.

Now add faith to your belief and go get it!

**TAKEAWAY:** St. Mark 9:23 Jesus said, *"If you can believe, all things are possible to him that believes."*

What are you worried about?

#OGHBYRG

# DAY 146: FACE YOUR GIANT!

Life can and will bring many challenges, but the reality is that if you back down or run from them, you'll be running for the rest of your life.

Before he became king, a man named David in the Bible was a shepherd. He had to face his giant! A giant that none of his older brothers were willing to face. Because David did something that his brothers were unwilling to do, David got something that they couldn't get!

I challenge you to face your giant today. Win, lose or draw you will make it through the challenge, and just like David defeated Goliath, you're getting ready to defeat yours.

**TAKEAWAY:** *"Is your giant really that big or did you make it appear to be?"* – Marlon Lock

#OGHBYRG

## DAY 147: IT'S LEARNABLE JUST REMAIN TEACHABLE.

Brian Tracy says, *"You can learn any skill you need to achieve, or any goal you want to achieve for yourself. There are no limits except the limits you place on yourself with your own thinking."*

Everything can be learned the question is, are you willing to put the time in and will you remain teachable? Never get to a point in life where you stop learning or feel you have all the answers.

If you want it, lets get it! Just be patient and remain teachable.

**TAKEAWAY:** You can learn from anyone.

#OGHBYRG

# DAY 148: HAPPY ANNIVERSARY!

Expressions to my grandparents on their anniversary (October 25th).

I know you both are with the Lord but there's not a day that goes by that I don't think about you both. Since today is your anniversary, I just want to wish you both a happy one.

I know y'all hanging out still doing your thing but know that I am still holding on to everything that you've instilled in me. I am instilling those values into my children and the church family.

You all be smooth. Thanks for watching over me, and we are still obeying God and God is still blessing us real good. I still feel you both with me today and forever.

**TAKEAWAY:** Never forget where you come from and never forget those who held you up when you couldn't stand by yourself.

#OGHBYRG

## DAY 149: YOU HAVE TO DO IT.

Whatever goals you're trying to reach, nobody's going to reach them for you.

Don't wait until next year to get it right. Next year is not even promised but today is!

So, I am challenging you to get better today. It's not that you don't know what to do, it's that you just haven't done it.

Mark Twain said, *"The only way to keep your health is to eat what you don't want to, drink what you don't like, and do what you don't feel like doing."*

**TAKEAWAY:** Get it done and just know that I am with you whenever you need that push.

#OGHBYRG

## DAY 150:
## IF WE TAKE THE TIME TO TEACH, THEY'LL TAKE THE TIME TO LEARN.

The Bible says, *"Train up a child in the way that he should go..."* If we don't train them up to be responsible, loving, God-fearing, great spouses, incredible parents, true friends, and loyal, then how can we expect them to know and do these things as adults?

When I look back over my life, I realize that everything that I learned was all apart of me being trained. What you see daily and talk about daily is what becomes a part of you.

The same way my granddad and my brother taught me, I make sure that I do that for others. I had the privilege of helping raise 2 of my brother's children. It was such a joy. To see them come into an environment that they were not used to was so cool to me. It was like they entered another world. The environment that they were in before coming to me was not bad, it was just different. My family did things differently than what they were used to and that's where the training took place.

**TAKEAWAY:** Someone took the time to show you, now you pay it forward by showing someone else.

#OGHBYRG

## DAY 151: IF YOU FAIL TO PREPARE THEN PREPARE TO FAIL.

It's real simple family, we must prepare.

Preparation always precedes a blessing. Many times, we wait until the opportunity presents itself, then we try to hurry and get ready for it.

At times you won't feel motivated and you won't feel like going the extra mile, but you must, with or without help, support and encouragement from others. You must be prepared.

**TAKEAWAY:** Always stay ready so you won't have to get ready.

#OGHBYRG

## DAY 152: GOD IS WITH YOU IN THE MIDDLE OF IT!

I love the Bible. I love learning how people before me had to endure the same things that I go through and they made it.

This let's me know that I am going to make it as well! One of my favorite passages of scripture is Hebrews chapter 11. It talks about faith, but most importantly the heroes of faith. These were people of God that acted on the belief that God was with them every step of the way. Or should I say God was, *"in the middle of it!"*

The same way God was with them, He's with you and I as well. Don't worry! God's got it all under control. He's in the middle of it.

**TAKEAWAY:** The substance is never on the surface it's always in the middle.

#OGHBYRG

## DAY 153: SOMETIMES YOU WIN AND SOMETIMES YOU LEARN.

These next 2 days are going to stretch you a little bit. I want you to know this in advance because I don't want you to think what I am asking you to do is asking too much, because it's not. I just really want you to dig deep and give more, even when it hurts.

So here we go. I want you to write out a list of everything that you failed at. I mean everything and don't hold anything back. I want you to then go back and try to put a date or timeframe on when these events happened. (this may take some time) For example, your age, what month, etc... This is to make it relevant again.

Then write down how you felt during each one of these failures. Be totally transparent and leave nothing out.

Finally, write out how you responded to each one of these feelings and emotions.

Now please understand something, you did not lose! You learned! You either win or you learn. That's the great thing about looking at life as a winner. Losing isn't even in your vocabulary.

**TAKEAWAY:** John Maxwell says, "You either win or you

learn."

#OGHBYRG

## DAY 154: THERE IS WORK TO DO.

What you did on yesterday for yourself, connect with someone today and do it with them. The same empowerment you felt on yesterday, someone else will experience that today. Now get to work.

**TAKEAWAY:** *"Don't look down on a man unless you're picking him up."* – unknown

#OGHBYRG

## DAY 155: ARE YOU REALLY DOING YOUR BEST?

Today you have to be totally honest with yourself.

I've learned over the years that it's easy for mediocracy to set in on this life journey. We can become complacent and lose that "edge," whether it's from failing in certain areas and allowing it to affect other areas, or whether it's reaching a higher level and feeling the work and effort can ease up a bit. Well let me help you. You should want to be the best you can be at all times in all things!

Not only you but your team as well. That's right, those around you should:

Make you better than you are.

Multiply your value.

Allow you to do what you do best.

Give you more time.

Represent you well.

Fulfill the desires of your heart.

If this isn't happening, are you really at your best?

I remember I was working out everyday, putting the time in

at the gym, but not in the kitchen. I was very strong, but I didn't have the look that I wanted because my diet was awful. One day I saw a photo of myself and it bothered me! I was totally embarrassed. What this photo did was made me look in the mirror truthfully at myself and make the necessary changes.

Let's look in the mirror today and tomorrow and see where we are, where we need to be, and get there! You got me pushing you the entire way

**TAKEAWAY:** Do your due diligence to eliminate anything toxic in your life. From food to relationships to bad habits. Be intentional and get it done.

#OGHBYRG

## DAY 156: EVERYONE IS AFRAID!

Don't let being afraid stop you from going after it.

Kill the mindset of being afraid by admitting that you are afraid, but you still are going to go after it!

It's your time, it's your season. Say: "Hello fear I am back!" That's right you are back and refuse to give up on your hopes and dreams.

The scariest thing in the world is to jump. We think of all the problems that can arise from the jump. But today think about victory and all the lives that will be changed because of your jump!

**TAKEAWAY:** Do it scared. *"If it wasn't worth it, you wouldn't be afraid."* – Marlon Lock

#OGHBYRG

# DAY 157:
# SET THE BAR HIGH AND KEEP IT THERE!

Your flesh will try to stand against you and get you to believe that you can do a little and still get a lot!

I think we've all been down that road at some point. We want high bar results but unfortunately, we don't want to put in high bar work! The mind will always tell you that's enough or there's an easier way. The reality is hard work pays off.

So what goals have you set for this year?

- I am losing weight
- I am reading the entire Bible
- I am going to find a church home
- I am going to save money
- I am going to build my credit up
- I am going back to finish my degree
- I am going to spend more time with family

Only to find yourself with 2 months left, and you haven't accomplished any of your goals. That may be because you really didn't set the bar high!

When you set the bar high you won't let anything not meet

the standard that has been set. In other words, you make no excuses!

We got some work to do family! Start now and when next year gets here, you'll be way ahead of the game!

Love y'all family.

**TAKEAWAY:** Set a goal that's unreachable and reach it!

#OGHBYRG

## DAY 158: THE GOD OF A SECOND CHANCE.

A young man at my ministry was falsely accused of something that he didn't do. He lost his scholarship and was humiliated all the while keeping his faith in God that God would bring him through!

It was rough. This young man had to go an entire year not knowing what would happen to his future, but he stayed true to the course and kept the faith as well as his innocence plea. Welp...

all charges were dropped, and he got his scholarship back and played collegiate sports again.

The same thing that God did for this young man is the same thing he wants to do for you!

Why? Because He's the God of a second chance!

**TAKEAWAY:** What will you do with your second chance?

#OGHBYRG

## DAY 159:
# EARTH HAS NO SORROW THAT HEAVEN CAN NOT HEAL.

In 2017 a gunman entered a church in Texas, shot and killed 20 people. Immediately I went into prayer:

*"Lord I ask you to comfort those in Sutherland Springs, Texas impacted by the senseless events today that took the lives of at least 20, including children."*

Although this happened last year, it still has such an impact on the present and future. The present because those lives that were taken - their families deal with it every single day. The future because we must pray in hopes that nothing like this ever happens again, although it has.

I am not sure what you may be dealing with but when you don't have the words to say, do not allow the issue to prevent you from trusting God.

**TAKEAWAY:** *"Sin will be rampant everywhere, and the love of many will grow cold."*

Matthew 24:12 NLT

#OGHBYRG

## DAY 160: YESTERDAY ENDED LAST NIGHT.

Let go of your past and focus on your today. This will set you up for your future.

It's so easy to live in the past.

Past mistakes

past hurt

past frustrations

past bad relationships

The reason you need to let go of your past is because it's crippling your future. You made it to see another day. Pick yourself up, dust yourself off, and wipe the tears away!

Go be great!

**TAKEAWAY:** Say this out loud, *"My today will be better than my yesterday and my tomorrow will be better than my today."*

#OGHBYRG

## DAY 161: WAR WHILE YOU WAIT.

Today I simply want to encourage you. Although you may be waiting for your next opportunity, phone call, email or a text regarding something that you desperately need, please don't just wait. War while you wait.

What does this mean? You can't just sit and do nothing! You are waiting but still be proactive in other areas. If you put all of your eggs in one batch and that batch was the wrong batch, then you are done! You lose focus you lose hope and you stop dreaming.

I am challenging you to plant seeds all over. Before you know it, doors and opportunities all around will open.

Keep fighting, keep pressing, keep believing in yourself! You got this.

**TAKEAWAY:** Just because you're waiting doesn't mean you stop fighting.

#OGHBYRG

## DAY 162:
## "PEOPLE WILL NEVER UNDERSTAND YOUR PASSION - IF THEY'VE NEVER EXPERIENCED YOUR PAIN." – MARLON LOCK

It's so easy to say what you would or wouldn't do regarding someone else's situation. The reality is that if you don't know a person's pain then you won't ever understand their passion!

When I resigned from the police force to become assistant pastor of the church my grandfather founded, it was one of the toughest things I'd ever had to do in my life!

I left a great career with the police department as a law enforcement officer and was newly married. I left during a painful season of my life. On top of leaving my career in law enforcement, I had to deal with the pain of seeing my grandfather suffer for years before passing away and then becoming senior pastor.

Then on top of that, I saw my grandmother, whose health deteriorated every year after my grandfather's passing. She still always smiled but the smile was different. Her smile also showed pain and the thought of, "How long do I have left."

Need I say, that these two raised me from 15 months up until adulthood.

What's interesting is the fact that my pain fueled my passion! I made up in my mind that I would be the best pastor that I could be and not let anything cause the ministry founded by my grandparents to fail!

People ask me why I do what I do and how do I do what I do. I simply say, "If you can't understand my pain, you'll never understand my passion."

**TAKEAWAY:** They may never understand why you do what you do, but when you do what God says to do, they don't matter.

#OGHBYRG

## DAY 163: SHOW UP FOR YOURSELF!

I've said and heard others say that what they do is for others.

I want to challenge you to think about yourself. Sometimes you just need to do something for yourself for a change. Think about it. As adults, especially with families, usually we are always putting others before ourselves. This is a great gesture and very commendable but what usually happens is frustration sets in and everyone is affected by it.

We do things to include others, but when you are so focused on everyone else, you can lose yourself, which causes you to be frustrated and feel under-appreciated.

I am challenging you to show up for yourself. Once you do it for yourself, with or without anyone or thing attached to it, it'll still get done!

Congrats to each of you in advance.

**TAKEAWAY:** Pick a day and set aside 4 hours just for you. It could be the gym, a spa day, going to dinner and a movie, whatever. Just take the time to show up for you. You deserve it. Live your best life.

#OGHBYRG

## DAY 164: HAPPY BIRTHDAY GRANDMA.

Man, do I miss my Grandma Lock. She was the sweetest woman that I've ever known. So considerate of others and the glue to our family.

My granddad (Paw Paw) was cool, but was *"moody,"* which means depending on his "mood" was how the day went for everyone (lol), but my grandma was consistent and so loving to everyone, no matter what. I think about her often.

Here's a note I wrote to her after her passing, on her birthday.

*"Hey Grandma, I've been in class all day but please don't think I forgot about your birthday. Today you would've been 87 years old. I know you and paw paw up in heaven doing y'all thang! Just know I think about you everyday. And Kim's (my sister) banana pudding is almost as good as yours I love you a whole bunch. Gone but never forgotten."*

Takeaway: My grandma would tell me after every mistake I made, *"Son, there's a brighter day ahead."* I am telling you this the same thing.

#OGHBYRG

## DAY 165: LIFE IS LIKE PHOTOGRAPHY – YOU DEVELOP FROM THE NEGATIVES.

I want you to really pay close attention to today's life lesson.

In life we must understand that we become our best by what we go through. The negative things and hardships are what make us who we are. This is where we get our "grit" from! That's right!

Negative situations help you develop. Now nobody likes them, but we all will have to deal with them.

Put your boots on and let's get after it! You got this and just know I am with you all the way.

**TAKEAWAY:** David never would've defeated Goliath if he hadn't had those experiences with the lion and the bear.

#OGHBYRG

## DAY 166: BLESS YOUR ENEMIES.

This may be a rough one, but you still have to do it. Yep, you committed to go all the way with me for 365 days to be the best you that you can be.

You're probably like, "bless my enemies? Umm I don't think so." Trust me, I understand. I used to be the guy that if you didn't care for me, I let you know (in your face) that I didn't care for you either. What I learned was that I was allowing my enemies to control me.

I was allowing them to dictate my life because I was so consumed with avoiding them that I would avoid places where they would be.

One day after reading my favorite book in the whole wide world (Holy Bible), I realized that God prepares a table in the presence of your enemies.

What? Wait a minute! Ummm hold up. You mean to tell me that my enemies are a part of my blessing? So, if I do my enemies good, even though they do me bad, I get the blessing? I get the reward!

Child please, I immediately started telling the ones that couldn't stand me, "I love you and there's nothing you can do about it!" I encourage you to try it, it's actually very liberating.

**TAKEAWAY:** Psalms 23:5

#OGHBYRG

## DAY 167: SUPPORT HAS NO COLOR.

I just want to thank all the men and women for giving me so many items for our church's homeless event.

Some heard about it, reached out to me, and were truly a blessing! I thank God for connecting me with great people. Notice I said people. No specific ethnic background or religion, just people. I think we get too caught up in support from just our own people but not the human race.

That includes everyone!

I love the fact that I have a diverse set of friends and colleagues.

So, thanks for the support!

**TAKEAWAY:** Regardless of color or status be willing to support people in need.

#OGHBYRG

## DAY 168: HOW BIG DO YOU WANT YOUR TABLE?

This is a question that I asked my congregation one service. I brought out a big dinner table, my best silverware, you know, the one you never use - it's only for decoration, and a meal fit for a king.

One group of people were dressed in all black and another group with all white. The group wearing black represented the enemies. The group wearing white represented the "good" people.

We then set the table sat the "enemies" down. The "good" people served their enemies! What was the point?

I was demonstrating a scripture in the Bible where it talks about blessing your enemies. Then I asked a simple question. How big is your table?

Your struggles come during the preparation. War in the wait! The table is prepared in front of (before) your enemies. They will see the favor of God on your life and you will know it was only God. He will receive the honor and glory from everyone.

Look at it like this, the more seats at your table, the more blessings you receive.

**TAKEAWAY:** *"Thou preparest a table before me in the presence of mine enemies: thou anointest my head with oil; my cup runneth over." – Psalms 23:5, KJV*

#OGHBYRG

## DAY 169: THINK BEFORE YOU ACT.

Life has a way of throwing things at us. If not careful, we just react and worry about the consequences later. Trust me, I've learned the hard way.

You must think before you act. My brother Mike would always say, *"Little brother take 10 seconds, breathe and think before you respond to any situation especially a negative one."* I said, *"why?"*

He said, "Because if (you're) not careful you will respond too fast and it'll probably be the wrong response. Then you'll have to go back and apologize when you just could've thought about it before you said or did it."

Man, this helped me so many times and it still does today. See sometimes you need to respond with a "you need a hug." (lol) Now it sounds funny, but it works.

**TAKEAWAY:** Next time you want to respond right away take 10 seconds and chill.

#OGHBYRG

## DAY 170: IF YOU TEACH, THEY'RE WILLING TO LEARN.

I am so happy for all my spiritual sons who are walking down the path that I chose as a young man, to work in law enforcement!

They all had their ups and downs but taking time to love them, walk them through their mistakes and equip them with the tools they need both spiritually and naturally, I can truly say that I am a humbled mentor. I can't wait to see what God does next in their lives, and I feel the same way about you. Yes you! I may haven't personally met you or even spoken to you, but the fact that you are reading this book has connected us.

You know how many mentors I have that I've never met or spoken to? To name a few there's John Maxwell, Bishop T.D Jakes, Jim Rohn, Brian Tracy, Tyler Perry, Oprah Winfrey, Dr. Charles Stanley, and the list goes on. The key to my mentorship with these people is that I was willing to learn.

Remain teachable and once you learn it, teach it and pass it on. It will return to you full circle.

**TAKEAWAY:** Always be willing to learn. There are

lessons being taught to you everyday.

#OGHBYRG

## DAY 171: WHAT ARE YOU REALLY SAYING?

I am a thinker. All day everyday. I think of how I can be better. What can I do more of? What can I do less of? How can I grow my community and city? How can I teach better? Just thoughts.

The thought I ponder the most is how can I represent Jesus Christ and my lifestyle as a Christian the best way possible?

People may never pick up a Bible to read it, but best believe they will read you.

What is your book saying? Can someone read you and see the love of Jesus? Or will they read you and say, *"If you're a Christian they'll never be one!"*

I've heard people say, "Don't look at people, be your own person," but the reality is we as Christians are supposed to be a light. We draw non-believers to Christ by our actions and lifestyles.

Is your light on? Has your bulb went out? If so, change your bulb and turn your light back on. Someone is searching for you.

**TAKEAWAY:** Be who you say you are at all times.

#OGHBYRG

## DAY 172: PREPARE FOR WHERE YOU'RE GOING.

I want you to really be transparent with yourself today. Think about where you are and where you want to be. Now ask yourself, have you really prepared yourself or have you become complacent?

You can lie to me and everyone around you but it's hard to lie to yourself! When you look in the mirror every single day you see the truth! You see the real you! You see the you that's been talking a good game, but you also see the you that's not putting in the work.

What are we going to do? I'll tell you. We are about to prepare now for where we are going!

You must prepare mentally, physically, emotionally and spiritually to get to your next level! That's right, you can't stay here. You've been stuck here in park for way too long. Today we are switching gears and switching lanes.

You have somewhere to be and a short time to get there! Now let's get to it.

**TAKEAWAY:** Go shopping and get some new clothes. Your new position is waiting on you.

#OGHBYRG

# DAY 173: A LITTLE LOVE GOES A LONG WAY!

My wife and I took on 2 awesome additions to help out my brother and his children.

We didn't get paid to do it, and we didn't even need a thank you.

A little love goes a long way. In this upcoming week, go out of the way to make someone feel special! You'd be surprised how it'll impact their life and yours.

**TAKEAWAY:** Read St. John 3:16, it's the greatest love story of all.

#OGHBYRG

## DAY 174: LOVE PEOPLE!

Every year we have our church's annual Thanksgiving turkey drive. It's such a joy to help those who may have fallen on hard times. We have sponsors and volunteers that step up and love to give back.

When I tell you that God has blessed me to be a part of an awesome ministry and community, I truly mean that.

If you can find it in your heart to just love and help someone who can't help you, please do it. Meet them where they are.

**TAKEAWAY:** The next time you see someone in a bad place just know that it could've been you.

#OGHBYRG

## DAY 175: GIVE THANKS!

In the Bible it says, *"in everything give thanks,"* not for everything, but in everything. I am challenging you to today to find something to be thankful for.

I want you to intentionally look for something to be thankful for. It could be that you woke up this morning or the ability to blink or bend your fingers. It could be that you got some

good news from the doctor. Whatever it may be, find something and find it quickly to be thankful for. If you're thankful for some people in your life then call them as soon as you finish reading and tell them, "thanks."

**TAKEAWAY:** After you tell them thank you then tell them to get this book. You may be laughing but I am serious, tell them to get the book.

#OGHBYRG

# DAY 176: EAT WHAT YOU WANT!

Believe it or not, sometimes it's good to get out of the *"routine."* So today, go eat what you wanna eat!

You've been working out, bettering your physical as well as your mental self. Now go and enjoy. Enjoy what, you may be asking. Well let's see here. Ok, go get that buckeye brownie. Or maybe that cheeseburger with bacon, grilled onions and extra mayo. Or maybe that snickers candy bar. Whatever you have be sure to enjoy and tomorrow get right back on track.

**TAKEAWAY:** Does a Snickers really satisfy? If it does, then why was I still hungry after I ate it?

#OGHBYRG

## DAY 177: BE THANKFUL!

My favorite holiday is my birthday; April 26th just in case you want to get me a gift. My second favorite holiday is hands down Thanksgiving.

The smoked turkey, yams, and macaroni & cheese, and dressing with the cranberry sauce. All, I mean all, the desserts you can imagine. Football games all day long, and party games with family and friends are incredible!

Outside of all that, I love the fact that you get a chance to spend time with the ones you love.

Christmas is cool, but if not careful, we focus on the gifts instead of the real gift (family). Be thankful for what you do have, because one day it just may be gone.

**TAKEAWAY:** You don't have to be thankful, you get to be thankful!

#OGHBYRG

## DAY 178: GIVE YOUR FAMILY SOME TIME!

No greater feeling in the world than to be at home loving my family and them loving on me!

I say this because my life is extremely busy. I am not complaining and wouldn't change it for anything, but I do realize what's truly important, and that's my family. I've learned how to *"balance."* Balance is so key but many over look it.

With all the meetings and events that come up, I realize that I can't do them on my own and be an effective husband, and dad. I use the word effective because I don't want to be married, but my wife feels alone. I don't want my kids to hear how great I am for others but wasn't there to be great for them. So, I make sure I give my family some time. Make sure you are doing the same.

Family please take the time to enjoy your family. Time goes by fast, money can run out, things get old, but memories last forever!

**TAKEAWAY:** There's no place like home!

#OGHBYRG

# DAY 179: CHECK ON SOMEONE IN THE HOSPITAL.

You may be saying, *"I don't know anyone in the hospital,"* but I didn't say check on someone you know in the hospital. I said to simply check on someone.

When I was a little boy my granddad would take me to the hospital with him to visit others. I'll be honest, I did not like it the majority of the time. However, by the end of the visit, when we were walking back to the car, and that person in the hospital remained there, it put things into perspective.

My granddad would say, *"Son always check on people that can't check on themselves."* This stuck with me. I take my kids now to hospitals and senior living facilities just to go and hang out with some of the residents.

I love to see elderly people's faces light up just from a visit. It means so much to know that someone cares.

**TAKEAWAY:** Go and make somebody's day at the hospital. You may just see me and my kids there.

#OGHBYRG

# DAY 180: I SHALL RECOVER IT ALL!

Ok by now you realize that everyday is not going to be grand. You will have some days (many of them) where it feels like you're losing!

It's not going to feel good, it's not going to sound good, and it will not look good. Can I be super transparent? Ok, some of the losses that you will encounter will hurt. It's going to be rough. But can I give you some good news? You sure you want it? Can you handle it?

You shall recover it all!

You may be wondering what does *"shall"* mean. It simply means that everything that the enemy stole, or you gave away, you are about to get it all back! It is a promise.

Plan your party. Call your friends and loved ones and give them a save-the-date! Yes, prepare for what's about to happen for you!

The loss of money- you get back!

Broken family- you get back!

Peace of mind - you get back!

Joy- you get back!

Swagger- you get back!

Get ready because it's about to happen!

**TAKEAWAY:** Say out loud, *"I am getting it all back!"*

#OGHBYRG

## DAY 181: BREAK THE HABIT!

*"The chains of habit are generally too small to be felt until they are too strong to be broken."* – Samuel Johnson

Man, that quote is powerful and so true. All bad habits start off in little increments and then form into one's regular routine. Now, I don't judge people and what they do. I only look at the outcome. If what you're doing keeps leaving you with a bad outcome, then you may want to quit. I'm just saying…

Habits are learned behavior so the good thing about learned behavior is that it can be unlearned.

I challenge you today family to "break the habit!"

**TAKEAWAY:** *"If you don't break the habit now, it will break you later."* – Marlon Lock

#OGHBYRG

## DAY 182: DISCIPLINE WITH LOVE.

I remember my granddad disciplining me as a young boy. Sometimes I got spanked, we called them *"whoopings"* back then, and sometimes I was placed on punishment – a timeframe where I could not do some of the things I desired. I didn't like either, but I appreciated them both.

The spankings were because I did something so bad that just a talk wouldn't have shown me the severity. If I had to choose, I would prefer punishments because they made me sit and think about what I did and how not to do it again. Regardless of the type of reprimand, it was always, I mean always, done in love!

You will meet someone who's gotten off track or did something the wrong way in some regard. Whether it's marriage, parenting, on the job, in the church, etc. They need correction, but they need it done in love.

The Bible says in St. John 3:17, *"For God sent not his Son to condemn the world but that the world through him might be saved."* Let's put forth the effort today to bring somebody up instead of tearing them down.

**TAKEAWAY:** Anyone can tear down, but few can build up.

#OGHBYRG

# DAY 183: A DELAY IS NOT A DENIAL!

Yes, you want it now, but the reality is you must wait. Delay your gratification.

We ask God or whoever we want something from, and we will receive 3 answers: Yes, no, or wait. That's right, wait. Most people struggle with waiting. Why? We don't understand *"delayed gratification."* Just because it's delayed doesn't mean you will not receive it, it just means you can't get it now.

Look at it this way. What if what you want right now, you aren't ready to handle it? If you get it now (too soon) then it'll be no good to you or for you in the future. But just what if you wait for it and you better yourself so that when you do get it, you'll be mature enough to handle it?

**TAKEAWAY:** Hey listen, I know you want it now but just know it's coming, and I am with you the entire way!

#OGHBYRG

## DAY 184: BE SELECTIVE.

Pay close attention to this one.

What do I mean be selective?

You have so many things on your plate and trying to do them all has left you with nothing completed!

Here's what you do – take the top 5 most important things you need to get done, prioritize them from most to least of importance.

Then start with the most important thing until it's done. Next move to what is second in priority. This will allow you to feel accomplished and motivated for your next move. As Brian Tracy would say, *"Eat that frog."*

Success in any area is predictable. Need a life coach? Someone to guide you every step of the way? I know I did. Guess what? You have one. You got me.

**TAKEAWAY:** The worse word you can say is, *"multi-tasking."* All that means is that each night you go to bed with the same amount of paper work on your desk that you had the night before.

#OGHBYRG

## DAY 185: IRON SHARPENS IRON.

I went out to eat with some ministers. We had an awesome time fellowshipping and just loving on one another. It's so easy to get so busy with ministry (business) that if not careful, we forget to just love and enjoy one another's company.

I love how my church family challenges me, pushes me, fights for me, and holds me accountable; but most of all, loves me!

They may not agree with me all the time, but they trust me enough to know that I'd never lead them the wrong way. I love them and value their opinions as well. Any relationship that works must work both ways. Get around someone sharp and stay sharp.

**TAKEAWAY:** Take the time to invest in someone else, the return is priceless. And remember.......... Iron sharpens iron!

#OGHBYRG

## DAY 186: ENJOY THE KIDS!

With all that life brings, sometimes we as parents can get so caught up with structure, planning and the responsibility of parenting that we seem to forget that our kids just want to be kids.

This week enjoy the kids! Let them play a little longer (play with them), let them eat dessert first. Trust me, it'll make all the difference in the world!

A little love and affection will go a long way with anybody, especially a child.

**TAKEAWAY:** I don't want to grow up, I am a Toys R Us kid!

#OGHBYRG

# DAY 187: NEW EVIDENCE.

I know the original evidence said, *"you won't make it,"* but the new evidence says, *"yes you will."*

I am believing in the second message. The first message was, *"I am about to lose,"* but the second message is, *"I win!"*

Who's reading this right now?

You are! You want to know why? It's because you are a winner and you were given false evidence that you were losing. The new evidence has been presented. It says you will get back everything you lost and then some.

The first piece of evidence was inadmissible, that means it doesn't count against you. So, it doesn't even matter what it was not, look at what it is!

Now grammatically this was probably all wrong. But you winning is all right! Now go be great.

**TAKEAWAY:** You still got time to reach some goals this year! Let's get it!

#OGHBYRG

## DAY 188: GET INTO THE PRESENCE OF GOD.

In my life I always found myself wanting to be in the presence of somebody. I am a people person. I love people and enjoy gatherings of all sorts. The older I get, I realize that I was focused on being in the presence of the wrong people. I began to notice that the more I was around people, the less I heard from God. I decided to get into the presence of God more. How, you ask?

I spend more time reading my Bible. I spend more time in prayer. I spend more time in worship and my life has completely changed for the better. I still love people and interacting with people, but I intentionally spend quality time in the presence of God.

**TAKEAWAY:** Life can and will hit you at any given moment. So always make sure you have a safe place and that place is in the presence of God.

You can always run to God and feel safe. There's some stuff you can't get - until you get in His presence.

Love y'all family!

#OGHBYRG

## DAY 189: REJOICE!

Take today to just give God some praise for what you do have. If we can't appreciate what we already have, then why would we appreciate more? In fact, why would God give us more?

In the book of James 5:13b it says, *"Is any merry? Let him sing psalms."*

You have something that you can rejoice about. Despite the not so good, the good outweighs the bad. Get to rejoicing!

Have an incredible day!

**TAKEAWAY:** *"If you look for a problem, you'll always find it. What's ironic is the solution was right there as well."* – Marlon Lock

#OGHBYRG

## DAY 190: I WANT IT ALL BACK!

We serve an amazing God that wants to bless us beyond what we can even imagine. Stop having a *"pity party"* for past mistakes, and instead have a "praise party" for what's in store!

Let the devil know that you want all your stuff back! You want your:

Peace

Joy

Family

Smile

Finances

Now claim it in Jesus's name!

**TAKEAWAY:** The bully took it, but you grew from it. Now go get your stuff back!

#OGHBYRG

## DAY 191: DON'T DRIFT AWAY!

You've been focused, and you've fought hard to get back on the right track. Please don't drift away.

It's so easy to revert to old habits. Don't fall into the trap of *"for old times' sake,"* or *"man I deserve it this one last time..."* Please hear me when I tell you that it's a trap!

You been good away from them.

You been focused away from them.

Your kids see you more.

You manage your finances better.

Your relationship with God is better.

You see the fruit of your labor.

You have peace!

Don't drift away!

**TAKEAWAY:** Stay focused!

#OGHBYRG

## DAY 192: CREATE A NEW IDENTITY!

It's easy to stay stuck where we are in life.

If not careful, we stop dreaming and think life must be meant to be the way that it is. Or we say, *"maybe it's not meant to be."* Nope we're done with that person! Let's start today with a new identity, a new mind-set, a new outlook on life.

Trust me when I say you can do it. The reason I know is because I had to do it. I had to recreate myself and my thought process and outlook on life. Not only did it better me but upgraded everything that I am connected to.

**TAKEAWAY:** Say this out loud:

*"My today will be better than my yesterday and my tomorrow will be better than my today."*

Let's go family! I am with you all the way.

#OGHBYRG

## DAY 193: IT'S COMING!

Please take this day serious. Not that all the others were not but pay close attention to today. Why? Because it's coming.

What you've been working for is coming and it's coming fast. You started this journey 192 days ago and made it this far.

You cried, you got angry, you quit and restarted. You said, *"I can't do this anymore,"* then realized all the while you said you couldn't and you wouldn't – you did!

Here we are. It's your moment, it's your time! Once you get through this, the rest is easy!

Stay focused, stay humble, stay grateful and just know its coming.

**TAKEAWAY:** If you wait on the Lord, He shall bring it to pass!

#OGHBYRG

DAY BY DAY WITH LIFE COACH MARLON LOCK

# DAY 194: TRUE FRIENDS.

Growing up, I thought everyone was my friend. As a matter of fact, I called practically everyone my friend.

Even today, I see how social media puts so much emphasis on friends and likes. Everyone is trying to see who got the most friends or who got the most likes, but the sad truth is that you don't have that many friends.

You may have a lot of associates, but not friends.

A true friend:

Is there for you through good and bad times.

Will keep you accountable.

Will always tell you the truth.

Loves you for who you are while you're becoming who you are intended to be.

Checks on you.

Wants to see you succeed.

Is happier for you over the promotion than you are.

Now how many friends do you think you have?

**TAKEAWAY:** My granddad said, *"Son, if you get 3 true friends in life, you are winning."* Man, he was right.

#OGHBYRG

# DAY 195: IT'S OKAY TO BE DIFFERENT – NOT WRONG.

My wife and I teach our children that it's okay to be different from others.

You like what you like and don't let anyone ever make you feel like you need to change from what you like.

If someone doesn't want to be your friend because you do not share the same ideas or likes as they, you probably need to change your association. Our differences make us unique.

Never change who you are to fit in with someone else! Never!

My daughter India is extremely gifted and talented in so many areas from piano, to dance, to singing, to academics... like, she's incredible. I noticed how in certain environments she would *"dummy down,"* if you will, in order to fit in or not to seem smart. My wife and I nipped that in the bud immediately. We told her, *"You can bring someone up to your level, but you can never dummy down to them."*

**TAKEAWAY:** I wore mismatched cuff links one day and everyone thought it was cool. It was a mistake, but it worked.

#OGHBYRG

## DAY 196: ENJOY LIFE! IT'S SHORT!

Every year our church has *"Ugly Christmas Sweater Sunday."*

One of our youth leaders, Edric Brunson, started wearing what the youth wore and it was super cool! All the young men admired Edric and wanted to mimic him. It spread like wild fire throughout the church. Now we all do it!

I know it's not common, but it's fun and we at Unity Gospel House of Prayer love it!

I am telling you that it's okay to enjoy life and have fun!

**TAKEAWAY:** The next time you go out to dinner. Order dessert first.

#OGHBYRG

## DAY 197:
## BE YOU – EVERYONE ELSE IS ALREADY TAKEN.

You have something in you that nobody else does. It's something that you bring to the table that others need. So be you!

Don't try to be like anyone else but who God intended for you to be. Admire others and recognize them for their giftedness and successes but don't try to be like them. Be you, because you rock!

**TAKEAWAY:** I tried walking bow-legged in middle school until I almost fell. I walk straight now.

#OGHBYRG

## DAY 198: WHAT WILL YOU SACRIFICE?

Sacrifice means you must give up something.

Many people want different results but are not willing to give up what's holding them back. Maybe this will help. I wanted peace in my life, that's it, just peace. My life was all over the place. I had things, but no peace. The things that I had were causing me not to have peace.

Guess what I did?

I sacrificed the lifestyle I was living for a better and new way of living. I sacrificed the world to follow Jesus.

What are you willing to sacrifice to get what you want? Well go do it. See you tomorrow.

**TAKEAWAY:** If it's easy, is it really a sacrifice?

#OGHBYRG

## DAY 199: DADDY AND DAUGHTER TIME.

I love when my big baby comes home, although she is going to ask for money, it does my heart good to know that she's headed in the right direction.

Listennnn, we've definitely had our ups and downs, but the love has always remained the same. I was very hard on my daughter, but it was done in love. I love it when she tells me how much she appreciates the discipline and structure we gave her. I showed her how she was supposed to be treated and what to see in her future husband in years, yes years, to come.

I used to push her, now she pushes me. I love my family and what God has done, is doing and getting ready to do in our lives.

Don't ever give up on your children. Invest in them today and they'll invest in you on tomorrow.

**TAKEAWAY:** To Tone'y you are the oldest, but you will always be my baby girl. You will have an amazing life and lead many souls to Christ.

#OGHBYRG

## DAY 200: BE UNSTOPPABLE!

*"If you are not willing to learn, no one can help you. If you are willing to learn, no one can stop you."* – Zig Ziglar

Zig Ziglar is one of the best authors of all time. This statement speaks volumes to humanity in every way. Anyone can change for the better if they would just be willing to learn.

Every day should be a day where you get a chance to learn, as well as share what you've learned with others. Never become the person who knows it all. If you do, you'll die with all you know and no legacy to carry it out.

Be a sponge for knowledge and become unstoppable!

**TAKEAWAY:** It's okay not to know. It's not okay not to know and act like you do.

#OGHBYRG

## DAY 201: IT'S JUST THEIR OPINION!

You are getting ready to embark on some amazing breakthroughs and opportunities. You have so much going for you from the decisions you've made each day. This is what I need you to do:

Stop stressing out over someone's opinion about you. If it's false, pray for them that they get help with that jealous spirit on them and if it's true and you feel the need to change, then change. But whatever you do, stop stressing!

Life is way too short and you'll never know a person's "true" opinion about you. So just always be true to what you believe in and be true to yourself.

Love y'all family.

**TAKEAWAY:** Stress kills, so don't stress.

#OGHBYRG

## DAY 202: SO PROUD OF YOU!

Our church had its first Christmas stage play and everyone was so excited! We had auditions, lights, props, I mean you would've thought Tyler Perry was putting this play on.

Well I happened to be on the selection committee and guess who auditioned? My mom! Omg....

So I am saying to myself, *"Mom, please don't be terrible because I am going to have to tell you that you were!"* Lol!

My mom walked in and she was really good. I mean really, really, really good! I couldn't show too much emotion because I didn't want to seem biased. So, I said, *"That was pretty good Ms. Lock, next."*

After auditions ended, my mom called me and was wondering my thoughts. I simply said, *"Mom I am so proud of you."* Not only was I proud, but on Christmas day, she nailed it!!

Why am I sharing this? Well it's my book so I can (lol), but I just want to encourage you to reach out to someone today and let them know how proud you are of them. It may mean nothing to you, but it will mean everything to them.

**TAKEAWAY:** If you have a choice to select your mother for anything, always select your mom. You only get one.

#OGHBYRG

## DAY 203: EVERY CHILD DESERVES TO SMILE.

My wife and I have 5 incredible children that we love with all of our heart. Everything that we do, we have them in mind because we know somehow, they'll be affected by the choices we make.

We do our best to make good choices, so they can be exposed to good, positive things. What does it for me, is to see the smiles on their faces; not smiles because they got something, or we are doing something fun; but just the fact that they are happy, full of joy and blessed beyond measure in the Lord makes it all worth it.

I love to see them watch how I interact with their mother. I love to hear them tell me how well they thought I brought forth a sermon, or how when I walk in the house they run and hug me and ask how my day was.

Tone'y says, *"Hey dad."*

India says, *"What's up big fella."*

Asia says, *"Where you been dad?"*

Sydney says, *"How was your day dad?"* Then tells me her entire day before I can answer.

Bro bro (Marlon 2) says, *"What you bring for me dad?"*

As each one is greeting me in their own way, they have the biggest smiles on their faces. There's nothing like seeing a child smile.

**TAKEAWAY:** Children already must deal with life, don't make them have to deal with you. Make sure you make them smile.

#OGHBYRG

## DAY 204: GOD FIRST!

Normally, we go out of town for Christmas; Thanksgiving always at home, and Christmas always somewhere warm. On this Christmas we decided not to go anywhere.

We just played around the house, had fun, ate desserts, did karaoke and decided to go see the movie Pitch Perfect 3. After the movie we went to the restaurant, Uno's Pizza. Here is where it gets good:

This young lady named Olivia (our waitress) was awesome! The Lord put on my heart what to give her for a tip, so I asked my family. They each gave an amount and I said, "Consider she's working on Christmas."

I asked Olivia how it felt working on Christmas. She said, *"I was given a choice. I could either work Christmas Eve or Christmas Day. I chose Christmas day because I didn't want to miss church on Sunday which was Christmas Eve."* Then she said, *"At least I have a job."*

My heart was overwhelmed because Olivia got it! See understands that everything has to come after God! Needless to say, it was a blessing for my family to be a blessing to this young lady.

I challenge you to put God first in all you do! Just like Olivia, you have a choice. Choose wisely.

**TAKEAWAY:** St. Matthew 6:33 read it.

#OGHBYRG

## DAY 205: VALUE YOUR TIME.

We must learn how to value our time.

John Maxwell gave me some great tips a couple years ago that I practice faithfully.

I look at my calendar and see all the dates and engagements that I took and ask myself, "Was it worth my time?" It's easy to forget what's most important.

We can get so busy being busy that what's truly important is left to struggle.

For example, I am grateful for ministering opportunities. However, I had to realize that if I preach at my ministry 3 to 4 days a week, and then take on other engagements the rest of the week, where's the time for my family? Where's the time to rest? Where's the time for me?

I've learned the value of my time. If you don't set your calendar, then someone else will. To those who feel like you have to grind and make it happen and your wife and kids understand, well blessings to you and I'll pray your strength.

My wife and kids love me at the house. I am not saying I am right, but I am saying do what works for you and value your time. Check your calendar and see how you could've made the best use of your time.

Love y'all family.

**TAKEAWAY:** You can never get back time, so don't waste it.

#OGHBYRG

## DAY 206: CONTINUE TO DO YOUR BEST.

It's so easy to compare yourself to others. Especially with social media and technology. It's easy to get caught up in trying to be like others, when your biggest competitor should be in the mirror.

Never do what you do for the people, always do it for you. The joy that comes from knowing God is pleased, your wife and kids are well taken care of, and you're doing it the right way, makes it all worth it. Continue to do your best family.

**TAKEAWAY:** There will always be flies on the wall. Just leave 'em there.

#OGHBYRG

## DAY 207: ALL YOU DO IS WIN!

I want you to say that out loud as loud as you can! All I do is win!

You got knocked down but you got back up – all you do is win!

You got knocked down again but got back up even stronger- all you do is win!

You were counted out but now they count on you – all you do is win!

You used to be the borrower but now you are the lender – all you do is win!

You were told you're not smart enough, good enough, attractive enough; so you got the degree, got your own business and got options to choose from- because all you do is win!

Keep winning!

**TAKEAWAY:** You win even with bad hands!

#OGHBYRG

## DAY 208: STRETCH YOURSELF.

Don't get all nervous from the thought for today. I am going to challenge you to do something you've never done to get something you've never had.

I am going to share with you why most people don't like stretching themselves. It's really simple. It's because they are used to being who they are and doing what they do.

Stretching is changing, and most people don't like or want to change, even if they need to.

I know I didn't. I was comfortable in my daily routine and just took life as it came until I realized I wanted better. Not just for me but it really kicked in when I got married and had a family depending on me. One day I had to make the choice to stretch myself and get better as a person, to better what was connected to me.

I told myself that for 21 days in a row, I would commit to reading growth and development books and apply what I read. Years later I am still on my 21 days. How? It became a habit.

What I learned in just 21 days changed my whole life around for the better. The same will happen for you, but only if you're willing to stretch just a little bit.

**TAKEAWAY:** I've always heard, "It's worth the wait." I say, "It's worth the stretch."

#OGHBYRG

## DAY 209:
## I MISS MY GRANDDAD.

Ok, here we go...

Words can't begin to express what this man still means to me even today. My granddad is the greatest man I've ever known besides Jesus.

This man imparted in me and never gave up on me, when he could have on many occasions. I didn't post last year on his birthday because I got so emotional just thinking about him.

I still cry often and still have my moments where I would just like *"5 more minutes."* I know he'd give me some great advice or tell me a really cool story about how it is on the other side. Through it all, I wipe the tears and think about how he's looking down on me smiling, giving me his approval fist pump, to let me know I am doing a pretty good job. I am not as good as him, but I am working on it.

I'll end here because I am about to cry. Paw Paw, thanks for never giving up on me and seeing something in me that I never saw in myself. Tell grandma I love her, and my clothes are still in her walk-in closet. Bro bro never met you, but he told me that he saw you before. (Bro bro is something else, so I pray he's not lying.) If he ever does get a chance to meet you in a dream/vision he'd remember. Sydney never met you either, but she would've had you wrapped around her finger.

I so love you my dude. Come visit me sometimes, I just need you to check on me every once in a while. Talk to you later, your son, "old tone cat."

Every time I write about him, talk about him or just think about him, I get so emotional. Man, I had the best granddad in the world.

**TAKEAWAY:** Gone but never forgotten.

#OGHBYRG

## DAY 210:
## YOU WILL SUCCEED BUT YOU MAY HAVE TO TAKE A DIFFERENT PATH.

Success is something that we all want, we all may not truly understand what success is or what it looks like. Each path looks different.

To one, success could be working for a Fortune 500 company. To another success could be a homemaker. To one pastor 10,000 members is a successful ministry but to another pastor 250 members is a success.

I don't know what success may be to you, but just know that you are already a success!

**TAKEAWAY:** No need for stressing over results; stick to it and it will happen.

#OGHBYRG

DAY BY DAY WITH LIFE COACH MARLON LOCK

## DAY 211:
## IF YOU QUIT - YOU LOSE!

Come next year this time you will:

Be financially stable.

Have a better marriage.

Have stronger relationships.

Have children performing better academically.

Have children with better attitudes.

Be at your desired weight.

Be promoted on your job.

Be the owner of your own business.

Be buying that rental property.

Be a better mother.

Be a better dad.

Be a better person.

Be on fire for the Lord.

All if you don't quit!

**TAKEAWAY:** If you quit – you lose!

#OGHBYRG

## DAY 212: YOU ARE NEEDED.

Yes you! You may play a small part, but that part is so important, and nobody plays that part like you. I mean nobody.

Don't ever not see your worth and the value that you bring to everyone and everything that is connected to you. You may be a dish washer, mail carrier, musician, a child, a street sweeper, an usher, a janitor...whatever you do, don't ever forget that you are needed!

**TAKEAWAY:** Whatever role you play regardless of how big or small, you are still needed. Never look down on the gift you have been given. Do your best with the little and watch how God multiples it!

#OGHBYRG

## DAY 213: SEE IT WHEN YOU CAN'T SEE!

The Bible says, *"Where there is no vision the people perish."* – Proverbs 29:18

You never become stuck because of the absence of things, it's always because of the absence of vision. Therefore, I need you to see it when you can't see it!

Look a little harder. Dig a little deeper. Dream a little bigger! It's right there in front of you. Don't miss it. Don't walk over it! Reach down inside of you and grab it and put it to use. You got this family.

**TAKEAWAY:** The acorn on the ground is stepped on and overlooked. They didn't know that it would one day become an oak tree.

#OGHBYRG

# DAY 214: JUST JUMP!

You're right on the verge of your biggest breakthrough yet!

You've prayed for it!

You've fasted for it!

You've put the time, energy and effort into it!

Don't let fear stop you... Jump!

You may think: "What if I go for it and don't get it?" I would counter that by saying: "Imagine what life will be like once you do!"

You must change your thought process! How we think and see ourselves is what we actually become.

I see myself as the best husband and dad in the world. I see myself as the best pastor with a thriving congregation of at least 10,000 members. I see me and my wife filling up auditoriums across the world talking to people about life, family, and marriage! I see me and my wife both on the New York Times bestsellers list!

Now you may say that you don't see that, but I am not concerned with what you see about me. I know how God sees me! I know the thoughts that God thinks towards me and the thoughts that He thinks of you as well.

That's why I jump! I already know that I will have a soft landing.

**TAKEAWAY:** What you have been considering, someone else is doing. Now jump!

#OGHBYRG

## DAY 215: NO VISION = NO VICTORY!

Habakkuk 2:2, *"And the Lord answered me, and said, Write the vision, and make it plain upon tables, that he may run that readeth it."*

I love this story in the Bible. It clearly tells us how we must have vision. Our vision must be so crystal clear to us that when we write it, it is obvious to others and they connect with us to make it happen. Vision requires support!

My question to you is, what do you have on the inside of you that needs to come out of you, so that everyone can see it, then take it, run with it and change the world!

**TAKEAWAY:** You got the vision, now go get the victory!

#OGHBYRG

## DAY 216: YOU HAVE AN ASSIGNMENT!

You have been given some type of an assignment, and until you complete it you can't pass!

If you do not pass, you are stuck where you are. If you get stuck where you are then those depending on you get stuck as well. What am I saying?

Do the assignment!

You know exactly what it is that you need to get done or get started. It's your assignment. It could be your children, your spouse, a friend, or a co-worker. You know that thing in your life that's assigned to you. Some of you are working on jobs where you don't want to be, but the reason you are there is because you have not completed the assignment that you were given for the job.

Get to work.

**TAKEAWAY:** Once you complete the assignment you pass the test.

#OGHBYRG

# DAY 217: GOD IS FAITHFUL!

When I was younger, I looked forward to spending time with my grandparents.

Whatever they told me would happen, I knew for certain that it would.

Now I have the same feeling about the Lord. He always keeps His promises because He is faithful! Since the Lord is faithful to us, we must make sure that we are faithful to Him. Even when others stray, you make sure you stay true to the course.

**TAKEAWAY:** *"He who promised to do it is faithful!"* Stop listening to the no's and consider who told you yes already.

#OGHBYRG

## DAY 218: FORGIVE.

It is so easy to look down on someone when they have done something wrong, but please keep in mind your shortcomings.

I am not saying to give them an excuse, but I am saying give a little grace. Think about when you messed up and how God granted grace to forgive you.

Look to forgive someone else. Don't be a part of the problem, be a solution to the problem.

It's so easy to tear down but you feel so much better when you build up.

**TAKEAWAY:** It takes the bigger person to forgive.

#OGHBYRG

# DAY 219: SHOW UP!

We all have had some type of membership to something that would get us in shape physically – or that treadmill in the house that turned into a clothes rack.

We purchased the membership to get in shape, but we didn't *"show up"* to the gym, so naturally we didn't get the results we wanted.

Then we purchased a treadmill and said, *"It'll be much easier to just work out at home. It'll save money and time."* Does this sound familiar? Only to not "show up" to the home treadmill and now it's a storage area.

If not careful, this behavior can carry over into other areas in your life where you just don't *"show up."* I am challenging you today to make the choice to "show up" and do what needs to be done. You got this!

**TAKEAWAY:** *"90% of success is showing up"* – Dexter Yeager

#OGHBYRG

# DAY 220: DREAM

I love dreams! I love how you can be asleep and while sleeping you can end up in other places.

I also like day dreaming and allowing myself to be who I want to be and to go wherever I want to go. I used to dream a lot as a kid but as an adult with life, and all it brings, I found myself only focusing on my realities.

One day I decided to start dreaming again. Never lose your dreams, but turn your dreams into realities. One of the greatest dreams I ever heard was that of Dr. Martin Luther King Jr, so, in honor of him…dream!

**TAKEAWAY:** I too have a dream - that all mankind will be saved. Amen

#OGHBYRG

## DAY 221: YOU'VE PLANTED – NOW WATCH IT GROW!

You have been putting the time as well as the work in for 220 days now and we arrive at day 221.

221 days ago, you planted something. You planted your resources to purchase this book and your time. Since then you have been watching it grow. Here is the issue with watching something grow: It takes forever, to you, but not to others. Others are seeing your growth much more than you are. They knew what and how you were, and they can see the change in where you are today!

Every time they see you, they see growth. I am challenging you to keep growing.

I know you want what you've been praying about right away, but the reality is you must wait.

Will you get frustrated? Yes.

Will you feel like quitting? Yes.

Will others get theirs before you? Maybe

But guess what? What you planted is still growing in the process. So, hold on a little while longer.

**TAKEAWAY:** *"Be intentional, growth doesn't just happen."* – John Maxwell

#OGHBYRG

## DAY 222: SIBLING RIVALRY

I remember growing up always wanting to beat my older brothers in whatever we competed in. Me being the baby boy, I was always looked upon as the weakest link. Not out of disrespect, but out of the fact that being the youngest I needed the most attention from the adults.

I couldn't go places my brothers went. I couldn't stay out as long as they did. I couldn't even stay up as late as them. I was pampered, and they took every opportunity to tease me about it.

They gave it to me and pushed me to be better as a child, and I carry that push with me until this very day.

Sibling rivalries are good and should be looked on as such. You need to push your sibling because society is going to.

So here I am today:

Both my middle school girls made it as finalists in the state-wide school spelling bee.

The only 2 African Americans to make it. This is great friendly competition, and I celebrate them for their achievements. I also celebrate their mom, my beautiful wife Kimberly, for pushing them and being the best example possible.

**TAKEAWAY:** Push your siblings to be better than you and when they reach that point, celebrate them like never before.

#OGHBYRG

# DAY 223: ISSUES

Nobody wants them but we all have them. Issues. What do you do when life sends you issues?

You handle them. You handle them as quickly and effectively as possible. Don't try and take the short cut. Tackle them straight on! Look that issue in the face and speak to it. Let the issue know that power belongs to God! Let the issue know that you have a solution to whatever problem you are faced with.

We all deal with issues, but the problem is that we hold on to them when we should let them go.

**TAKEAWAY:** *"Everything created is a solution to a problem." –* Mike Murdock

#OGHBYRG

# DAY 224: BE A LEADER.

Are leaders made or born? I've heard this question asked so many times. I personally feel that leaders are born but need to be taught "how to" lead.

I think we all are leaders in some regard, but many choose not to lead.

My son was not feeling well and wanted me to carry him. I told him, *"A true leader carries the load even when they don't feel good."* He cried, wiped his eyes, and kept it moving.

I am telling you to do the same. You are built for it, now lead; not by words but by your actions.

**TAKEAWAY:** It's never too late to lead.

#OGHBYRG

# DAY 225: LET IT RAIN!

Growing up I couldn't stand when it rained. I thought my day was all messed up.

I couldn't go outside because my mom would not want me tracking rain and mud in the house. Or she would say that playing in the rain would get me sick. I couldn't go to the park. I couldn't ride my bike. I did not like the rain.

One day I was with my granddad and it started to rain, and I put my sad face on. My granddad said, *"What's wrong son?"* I told him how I didn't like the rain and how the rain messed up everything. He looked at me and said, *"If you don't like the rain then you don't like to eat."* You can imagine as a kid the look on my face. I said, "I do like to eat," and my granddad said, "well you like the rain, because when it rains it grows the fruits and vegetables that we eat." This messed me up. My granddad continued about how important the rain was.

As I grew older, I never forgot the importance of rain as well as storms. Storms may seem crazy, but they still bring forth growth. The storm that you are in right now, is developing you into the person you need to be. So, let it rain.

**TAKEAWAY:** *"Can you stand the rain."* – New Edition

#OGHBYRG

## DAY 226: RENEWED MIND.

I often heard my granddad minister and talk about renewing your mind. I would wonder: *"How can you renew your mind?"* As I grew older, I realized that each day you must start out with a new mind set or new outlook on life. What was a struggle for me on yesterday will not be a struggle for me today. It's all in the renewing of your mind.

Please don't ever let what you can't do, keep you from doing what you can do.

Family – let us renew our minds. If we do not renew our minds, then we prevent the Spirit of God from doing the transformation process.

*"And be not conformed to this world: but be ye transformed by the renewing of your mind, that ye may prove what is that good, and acceptable, and perfect, will of God."* – Romans 12:2 KJV

**TAKEAWAY:** Say this out loud, *"My today will be better than my yesterday and my tomorrow will be better than my today."*

#OGHBYRG

# DAY 227: TAKE RESPONSIBILITY.

You fell off the wagon, got back on it and now you've fallen again. So...get back up again.

You thought life would be easy? You think life is a game? Please listen to me! Life is tough and comes with so much responsibility. All you have to do is be responsible. That's the key to life, being responsible. Responsibility is a choice. You either choose to be responsible or you do not.

Just don't blame others.

If I told you how many times I have failed, you would probably stop reading this book. What you may not realize is that I got back up again every single time!

I failed at my first marriage

I failed in relationships

I failed in college

I failed in my integrity

I failed as a dad

I failed as a friend

I failed as a husband

But I never quit! I took responsibility for my actions and

found a way to win and you are going to do the same thing! I refuse to let you stay in that low place! Get up and go win!

**TAKEAWAY:** You want better? Go get better!

#OGHBYRG

# DAY 228: SOMEONE IS WATCHING YOU.

Hey family. Be aware of the choices you make. They can and will affect someone around you.

I have this picture of a small boy surrounded by 4 adult men. It reminds me of how children and others want to be just like the adults they are surrounded by. All the little guy knows is that he is hanging with the big guys. He can't articulate like them. He can't understand like them. He can't do what they can do. He can't drive. He can't call and place an order for food, there are so many things he cannot do. The one thing the young boy can do is watch what the adults are doing.

**TAKEAWAY:** Be responsible today family, always do what you know is right because someone is watching.

Quentiel, your son will be great because of a dad like you.

#OGHBYRG

## DAY 229: ANNIVERSARY

Words cannot express the emotion that I have. I am literally all over the place, but it's a good place. I am so grateful to God to be able to oversee a ministry that has been around since 1973; not just around but effective and all the glory belongs to God.

I know my grandparents (founders) are smiling. Yeah, that's pretty cool.

To God, I thank you for choosing me to do what you have ordained me to do. I'll continue to lift your name on high and lead by example. Thank you for the people that have come and are connected to the ministry.

**TAKEAWAY:** I don't have to be a pastor, I get to be a pastor.

#OGHBYRG

## DAY 230: THERE'S STILL WORK TO DO!

Achievements are great, to be recognized for those achievements are pretty cool, but there is still work to do.

Enjoy those moments and allow them to drive you even more to continue. It is so easy to become complacent, not realizing there is always more to give. More lives to impact. More lives to touch.

Where you are right now is only the beginning. It's just a sneak preview of the incredible things to come.

**TAKEAWAY:** *"Everyday plant a seed and everyday expect a harvest."* – Pastor Marlon Lock

#OGHBYRG

## DAY 231: EVERYONE IS AFRAID.

Ralph Waldo Emerson says, *"Do the thing you fear, and the death of fear is certain."*

I think everyone gets afraid at some point or another. That is just a part of life, or should I say human nature. You cannot let that stop you from reaching your goals!

Use it to your advantage. Turn that nervous energy into a weapon. Go all out and explode while doing it. Every successful person you know was afraid at some point.

**TAKEAWAY:** The way you overcome your fears and develop unshakable levels of courage and self-confidence is to deliberately do the very thing that you fear, over and over, until the fear is gone.

#OGHBYRG

## DAY 232: "I FELL ON GOOD GROUND."

In the Bible there was a sower who sowed seed. Some of the seeds fell by the wayside, others fell on stony places, but some fell on good ground.

The seed that fell by the wayside was eaten by birds. The seed that fell on stony ground had no root and was scorched by the sun. But some seed fell on good ground and grew drastically!

What I am saying to you today is that if you happen to fall, make sure it's on good ground.

**TAKEAWAY:** You may have fallen but thank God that you fell on good ground! Now get up and see the salvation of the Lord!

#OGHBYRG

## DAY 233: NEVER STOP.

In life, it seems as if everything happens all at once. We don't deal with issues immediately, so they pile up and we feel overwhelmed.

To get rid of the "mess pile" you must never stop! That's right, it will take time to get things back in order, but the time you spend is well worth the reward. No matter how high the pile may seem, I encourage you to never stop.

You may do it with hands sweating.

You may do it with knees knocking.

You may do it with tears in your eyes.

You may do it with bumps and bruises.

No matter how you have to do it – never stop!

**TAKEAWAY:** *"It doesn't matter how long it takes you just as long as you don't stop."* – Confucius

#OGHBYRG

## DAY 234: SUCCESS BEGINS WITH YOU.

Dexter Yager says, *"Success begins by raising the opinion we have of ourselves."*

Man, I like this quote because it's so true. I want you to ask yourself a question. Yes, really talk to yourself. What do you think about you? Seriously ask yourself this question. If you don't think good about yourself then how can you expect others to? Actually, how can good come from you if you do not think good of you?

When we base our self-worth on what others think, we lose every single time. When we base worth on what we feel about ourselves, we always win. So, think yourself happy! Don't you go another day trying to please another person. Please God, take care of your family, and do right by people.

If you try to please everybody, be ready to live the life that everybody will plan for you.

**TAKEAWAY:** You are great at being you, so be great today.

#OGHBYRG

## DAY 235:
## TREAT HER LIKE A QUEEN WHEN SHE'S YOUNG; THAT'LL BE HER STANDARD WHEN SHE BECOMES AN ADULT.

I love all my children and want the best for them in every aspect of life; from spirituality, to schooling, to best friends, and potential husbands. To see the best manifest in them, I treat them the way they should expect to be treated.

I show them how a woman should be loved and cherished when they see me interact with their mom. I talk to them with respect and adoration, so they know how their future husbands should talk to them.

My job is to show them what to expect and look for. If they don't get it, then he is not the one.

Hanging out, loving on them, explaining to them how they are supposed to be treated, and teaching them to set that standard high now, means all the world to me.

**TAKEAWAY:** If you teach them, they will learn.

#OGHBYRG

## DAY 236:
## MAKE EVERY SECOND COUNT

Every second wasted is an opportunity wasted.

One goal I set for myself this year is not to let anything, or anyone waste my time.

If it cannot better me or I cannot make something else better, then it does not deserve my time or my energy.

**TAKEAWAY:** Make it count

#OGHBYRG

## DAY 237: I DON'T FEEL LIKE IT.

Boy have I said this many times in my life: *"I just do not feel like it."* It looked something like this when I was younger through adulthood:

Clean your room son – I don't feel like it

Take out the garbage – I don't feel like it

Wash the dishes – I don't feel like it

Do your homework – I don't feel like it

Get ready for work – I don't feel like it

Get to the gym – I don't feel like it

Invest your money wisely – I don't feel like

Now in my life as a husband:

I don't feel like struggling

I don't feel like stressing

I don't feel like being overweight

I don't feel like being around negativity

I don't feel like losing

I don't like coming up short

Everyday I crush the obstacles in front of me!

**TAKEAWAY:** *"It means more when you don't feel like it."*
– Pastor Marlon Lock

#OGHBYRG

## DAY 238: THERE'S A MIRACLE IN THE MOMENT!

Today you will have an opportunity to impact someone's life in a major positive way.

They are going to need you! God needs you as well!

There are some things that you have been through that they're going through. You can make their load lighter by letting them know - it gets better. Don't miss out on the moment to change a person's life for the better.

Your sacrifice to help someone else will continue to allow you to find yourself always getting through.

**TAKEAWAY:** *"Yesterday is gone. Tomorrow isn't promised; but today will be great."* – Marlon Lock

#OGHBYRG

# DAY 239: SURROUND YOURSELF WITH GOOD PEOPLE.

You can never reach where you need to be without good people. Not people who are just good in words, but good in action and character.

Surrounding yourself with good quality people is key to what you attract. So, I guess the question of who and what are you attracting is okay to ask here.

Are you surrounded by people who motivate and push you to better?

Are you surrounded by people who are happy when you succeed?

Are you surrounded by gossipers and complainers?

If there is something off balance, do what I did. Love people where they are. I love everyone, but foolery and negativity I will not be apart of. I am so grateful for the incredible people that God has placed around me. I am a better person in every aspect of life because of you. Thank you all.

**TAKEAWAY:** God has truly placed some amazing people in my life to help me on this journey. You can do okay alone, but you can reach heights you never imagined with a quality team.

#OGHBYRG

## DAY 240: KEEP CLIMBING!

I work out 6 days a week for several different reasons, but the main reason is I love new challenges. Whether it's in my body or my mind; carnally or spiritually, I love a challenge.

My biggest challenges in the gym were pull-ups and the stair machine. I hated them both!

When you talk about a burn, frustration and an attitude…do the stairs!

What gets me through a stair machine workout is that I see myself climbing up to my next victory or my next opportunity. I visualize my wife and kids rooting for me saying, *"You got this, just keep climbing!"*

This makes the climb worth it because it is not just for me. I have others depending on me to keep climbing. You do too. Don't stop, don't quit, and don't give up! You have too much depending on your climb.

**TAKEAWAY:** The only way you can not reach your goals, dreams, etc., is if you stop climbing.

#OGHBYRG

## DAY 241: BELIEVE IN YOU!

You must be your biggest supporter. I am not saying to make it all about you, but I am saying to believe in you.

You must have that "something" on the inside of you won't let you quit. I call it "get back." Once you get it, never lose it.

Remember the dream you had was for you not them! Believe in you! When I tell you that you got this, I am not just trying to pump and prime you, I truly mean it! I am just here to give you a little push. Now let's get it!

**TAKEAWAY:** People will believe in everything except your dream. Show them it wasn't just a dream!

#OGHBYRG

## DAY 242: REACH OUT!

Life may be great for you and yours but there is someone that needs you!

Never get to a point where you do not help others. Anyone in life that has reached any level of success had someone to reach out to them. There is someone that you are going to connect with, that simply needs your help. Help is not always financial. It could be emotional support, a listening ear, attendance to an event, feedback, strategy, prayer – just be willing and ready.

**TAKEAWAY:** Pay it forward.

#OGHBYRG

# DAY 243: ENJOY THE MOMENT.

When I look back over my life, I often think about all the people that were in my life and how over time they were gone.

I think about my dad and my grandparents. The moments that I shared with them. Then I think about how I sang at my dad's funeral service at the age of 10, and how I preached both my grandparents' eulogies.

I am emotional at times, but I usually recall the best moments that I shared with them.

We would take family trips every year from Wisconsin to Spartman, Arkansas for our family reunion. We would stop in Missouri at Boomland. We would visit my family that I didn't know that well but were family members my grandparents' grew up alongside. Every year they'd say, *"Wow you've grown."* Then we would eat, play cards, sit around and talk for hours. Trips like those taught me to enjoy the moment. You never know when that last moment will be.

I am challenging you to slow down and enjoy the trip. Take that walk in the park. Go to your child's recital or game. While there, enjoy the moment!

**TAKEAWAY:** I've always heard growing up, "Here today, gone tomorrow." It's true.

#OGHBYRG

## DAY 244: MAGIC MONDAY

Mondays are normally viewed as dreadful and slow days while Fridays are viewed as amazing! Why is this? One reason that we look forward to Fridays is because of the weekend, and Mondays are usually the beginning of the work week.

Let's change our mindset. Instead, let us view Mondays as new beginnings. You do know that Monday is not promised. You do realize that you do not have to awake in sound mind, body, and spirit…you get to start off strong and make your week incredible!

Make your Mondays so productive that your Fridays are jealous of them. Change your mindset, change your life!

**TAKEAWAY:** I'm changing the old song Just Another Manic Monday to Just Another Magic Monday.

#OGHBYRG

## DAY 245: WHAT ARE YOU ATTRACTING?

Many people complain about their circle of people.

They complain about home, work, the gym, the pub, their church... well you get the picture, right? These types of people complain about everyone and everything, but never pause to look at what they are attracting.

There is a reason why you have the "dead beat" person in relationships.

There is a reason why you don't like any job you have ever worked.

There is a reason why something is always wrong at every restaurant you go.

Consider this question: Are you attracting negativity because you speak negatively? Just maybe it's not everyone else. Maybe it's you.

Do yourself a huge favor. Take a look at what you are attracting and if it is not healthy for you, become unattractive to it.

**TAKEAWAY:** It's not always the other person.

#OGHBYRG

## DAY 246:
## DON'T FEAR – YOU GOT THIS.

Think of living a life where you had no fear.

Fear causes us not to pursue it.

I want you to think about one thing that was so heavy on your mind and heart to do but you let fear stop you from doing it. Think of all the lives that could have been changed and impacted all because you went for it! Think about the financial freedom that you could have for you and your family. Don't you think you at least deserve to give it a shot? I do. I think you should start dreaming again! Not only dream but pursue your dream. You have been dreaming for some time, but fear destroyed the dream. It is time for action.

You bought this book for a reason! Now apply what you have been learning and go for it!

**TAKEAWAY:** Start today.

#OGHBYRG

## DAY 247: COMMUNICATE THE RIGHT WAY.

Communication is such a critical part in life and everything that goes with it. If you can't communicate effectively, then your relationships on every level will be suffer and nothing will get accomplished.

A mentor once told me that, *"Clarity creates speed."*

Creating speed is critical to getting the job done timely and effectively.

What is also important with communication is that you cannot talk *"at"* a person. You must talk *"to"* them. Talk to them with the same level of respect that you desire.

*"Your communication can wound others or heal them."* – Steve Scott

**TAKEAWAY:** Proverbs 12:18 says, *"There is he that speaketh like the piercings of a sword: but the tongue of the wise is health."*

#OGHBYRG

## DAY 248: GIVE HONOR WHERE HONOR IS DUE.

I had a truly humbling experience. I was honored during a black history month program.

I was invited to a school and the students dressed up like famous black historians that changed the world. I was literally blown away to see a student dressed up like me, with photos, an image about who I am and what I am striving to accomplish.

I am grateful for my life and the gift(s) God has given me to help others. I have not even scraped the surface of what legacy I will leave, but I am definitely happy to be where I am.

I am a big cry baby, but I held it together in front of the kids. All I can say is, *"To God be the glory!"* Find someone today and honor them. No matter how small or great of a thing they did, they did something.

**TAKEAWAY:** What are you doing to bring honor to you and your family?

#OGHBYRG

# DAY 249: BE A MENTOR.

I see many young people who I am connected with, that are traveling the same paths that I did while growing up. I make it a point to connect with them and be some type of positive influence.

I am a firm believer that if you have made it through something in life, be willing to help someone else make it as well. If we had more mentors instead of critics, society would be better.

Let's not look down on the person making the mistake. Let's find a way to pick them up.

You can be a mentor in so many ways, and there are so many organizations that are looking for mentors to donate just some amount of time.

What if your experience helps someone not have to go through what you did? How cool is that!

**TAKEAWAY:** Find someone to pour into.

#OGHBYRG

## DAY 250: ARE YOU READY?

Ready for what, you may ask?

Ready for the door that is about to open up for you! That's right, you have been putting the work in so why not you?

Preparation always comes before a blessing. I read this one day, *"If I fail to prepare, I am preparing to fail."*

This is day 250. Don't you think it's about time for you to reap what you have planted? I think so. As a matter of fact, I know so.

Make sure you are ready for what is on the horizon and know that you deserve it!

**TAKEAWAY:** Preparation attracts luck, but you do know that you are not lucky…right?

#OGHBYRG

## DAY 251:
# WHAT DO YOU DO WHEN YOU DON'T FEEL LIKE DOING IT?

I just want to encourage you and let you know that you will not always feel like putting in the work towards what you are striving for. Do it anyway!

You will be tired but still do it!

You will get frustrated but still do it!

Folk will laugh at you but still do it!

It will feel like you are missing out but still do it!

**TAKEAWAY:** Go do it. Only people that don't reach their goals care about how they feel.

#OGHBYRG

## DAY 252: PAY ATTENTION!

Don't let life get you so busy being busy, that you stop paying attention.

Pay attention to your:

Wife

Children

Relationships

Business affairs

Health

Walk with God

**TAKEAWAY:** If you don't pay attention to it and give it life, it will die.

#OGHBYRG

## DAY 253: MAKE A POINT TO GROW.

Growth is something that we do each day. Just make sure that you are growing the right way.

Anything you let become a part of you can and will grow within you. When we grow, we must make sure that we are in the right soil as well as the right season. I don't have a garden, but I do know that there is a season to plant as well as a season to harvest what has been planted. I also know that you cannot plant in the winter and expect anything to grow.

Timing is everything. Today is the time for you to be intentional about your growth and development. Connect with a ministry, a mentor, or a positive club with individuals looking to better themselves.

**TAKEAWAY:** *"You only live once, why not live it to the fullest."* – Marlon Lock

#OGHBYRG

Bishop T. D. Jakes, thank you sir.

#pisgah2018

## DAY 254: TELL HER HOW MUCH SHE MEANS TO YOU.

I am not sure who the significant women are in your life, but please know that their value is worth more than gold.

When I look at all the incredible women that God placed in my life, I can say He outdid Himself. From my mothers and grandmothers, to my 4 daughters, and to all my sisters that God has placed in my life; they all play such a major role in my life.

Last but certainly not least, the most beautiful girl in the world, my wife. Words cannot express how my life was changed forever once she came along.

Male or female please reach out to a woman that has impacted your life in some way and simply say "thank you." Let her know how much she means to you.

**TAKEAWAY:** Tell her today because tomorrow is not promised.

#OGHBYRG

## DAY 255: HAVE A SYSTEM.

Having a system in place simply means you need to have structure.

Most people think they have structure, but the reality is they kind of just take things as they come.

I'll admit I am a great visionary, but I have incredible people on my team that make it all work. From my ministry, music, business endeavors, etc... I could not do what I do without the people in place that make the system work.

Take some time today to talk to the right people and ask the right questions to get a system in place for your life. I recommend connecting with one of the top 5 people in the industry you are in or seeking to enter.

**TAKEAWAY:** For you who have a system that is not working, let me help you... Get a new system!

#OGHBYRG

## DAY 256: THERE IS NO PLACE LIKE HOME.

I travel a lot. I have experienced some of the most beautiful places in the world!

I have climbed mountains, I've sailed the seas and ate some of the best food, but there is still no place like home. When I think of home, I have a sense of peace.

I am excited when the plane lands and I am rushing to baggage claim and then to find my vehicle. Once in my vehicle, I call and order my family's favorite meal, pick it up and surprise them when I walk through the door.

My daughters run and all hug me. My son walks up real smooth and says, *"What's up dad."* Then my wife greets me with a kiss (well usually), but man oh man does it get me every time.

My home is what I have made it. Whatever you want in your home you must put it there. Love, joy, peace, understanding, kind words, you must place it there because no home includes these invaluable things.

**TAKEAWAY:** Make your house into a home.

#OGHBYRG

# DAY 257: DAD, CAN I DO YOUR HAIR? SURE.

Ok, stay with me. My daughters (especially Sydney) love to brush my hair and oil my scalp. I mean she goes all in like I am at the beauty shop. She gets combs and brushes and hair oil and has at it and I allow her.

One day my mom stopped over and saw Sydney greasing up my hair and said, *"You know she got that from you right?"* I said, *"Got what?"* My mom said, *"Doing hair."*

Then my mom proceeded to tell me how I would do my dad's hair when I was a little boy.

She said one day my dad was asleep and I got a big jar of grease and put the entire container in his head. When he woke up his head was completely white. I said, "So what he do?" She said, "He just looked at me and smiled and said that boy something else."

I cannot remember that. What I can remember is the moments that I still share with all my children.

I lost my dad at age 11, what I wouldn't give to be able to put grease all in his head again.

**TAKEAWAY:** Life is short. Let your kid put grease in your hair. They just might be the next Madam CJ Walker.

#OGHBYRG

## DAY 258: ENCOURAGE SOMEBODY.

What up family, there's somebody, somewhere, putting in work doing the best that they can do. You will see them today.

They have been working so hard. Some have stopped working altogether but need a word of encouragement from you.

It's so easy to point out others' flaws but let's learn to point out their good points. The same way you find a way to complain, be sure to find a way to compliment.

**TAKEAWAY:** Put a crown on someone's head today.

#OGHBYRG

## DAY 259: SEEK WISE COUNSEL.

It's so easy to want to go at it alone then sit back and look at what you accomplished. That is great that you have a mind set of *"making it happen,"* but hear me please..........

Don't try to make it happen by yourself. Seek wise counsel. Get in the room with some people that can push you closer to your vision. Get into a room where you are not the smartest or most intelligent. Get into a room where you feel intimidated and soak up of every bit of information that you can.

*"Without the aid of counsel, you will fall."* Proverbs 11:14

**TAKEAWAY:** You don't have all the answers.

#OGHBYRG

## DAY 260:
## BE WISE IN A FOOLISH WORLD.

Each day you will have an opportunity to decide. Not a forced decision but a free-will decision and I want you to choose wisely.

I tell my children all the time that I am not concerned with how other families do what they do. My responsibility is for my family. I tell them to never make a decision upon someone else's beliefs or opinions.

Always do the right thing because it is right. I also tell my children to be the friend to that kid everyone else picks on. Don't join the bullies! Be wise.

What is wisdom? Wisdom is simply knowing the difference, that's it. Know the difference between right and wrong and choosing to do right.

**TAKEAWAY:** Before you do anything, please think about what you are about to do.

#OGHBYRG

## DAY 261: WHEN IT GETS YOU DOWN, GET BACK UP.

Anyone that has ever been great at anything had to deal with being knocked down.

Knocked down because you were told you were not good enough.

Knocked down because of your level of education.

Knocked down because of your past.

Knocked down because of your ethnicity.

Knocked down because of your will to not be a follower.

Knocked down because of jealousy or the *"crab"* mentality.

Whatever the reason was, it's not cool to be knocked down, but do you know what is so awesome about you? You always get back up! Now give yourself a pat on the back and go be fabulous!

**TAKEAWAY:** I get knocked down 7 times, but I stand up 8.

#OGHBYRG

## DAY 262: GIVE UP TO GO UP.

We all desire to get to that next level in some area of our life.

Most times we confess this next level desire with our mouths but not in our actions. The reality is, is that if you want to get better in any area, you have to give up something in another area.

You cannot get better at something new without being willing to sacrifice something old.

Let me explain it this way. What you are doing now requires time right? If you keep to the same routine, then where will the time come from for the next level?

I wanted to become a better pastor and leader, so I had to give up a lot of television to put the time into studying. Now you may say that's a bit extreme. Well I expect extreme results. What are your expectations?

**TAKEAWAY:** No sacrifice no reward.

#OGHBYRG

## DAY 263: BE POLITE AND ALWAYS SAY, "EXCUSE ME."

Manners are a form of conduct that seem to be lost in many situations. We fight and argue all because we have lost our manners.

I remember my mother and grandmother would always tell us boys to, *"practice good manners."* If we were ever given something, they would say, *"Did you say thank you?"* They were training us, and we didn't realize it. My grandmother would say, *"You know it costs nothing to be polite."*

Still to this day, I make sure I practice good manners.

**TAKEAWAY:** I challenge you to be polite to everyone because someone's always learning.

#OGHBYRG

## DAY 264: LIFE LESSONS.

My son cut his hair in school with scissors.

I am grateful that he is okay, but I expressed to him the severity of playing with scissors. I also expressed to him how bad things could be if he cut himself or accidentally cut someone else.

I asked a group of people on social media to give me some (parenting 101) tips.

Suggestions were:

Spanking

Verbal scolding

Punishment

Cut hair completely bald

Fall back; give him a pass

The majority said to give him a pass. I did just that and chalked it up as a life lesson. He was nervous about the repercussions, but no spanking, no punishment, I just had a heart-to-heart with him and let him know my thoughts.

**TAKEAWAY:** Use your life lessons as teachable moments. They go so far.

#OGHBYRG

## DAY 265: ACCOUNTABILITY

This is one of the most, if not the most, important things we all need in life.

That's right. Accountability. If we all had accountability, the world would be a better place and relationships would be more meaningful. One of the rules that I live by is having people in my circle to hold me accountable. I believe that if you have people in your circle that allow you to fail then how can they truly love you?

I don't need a friend to agree with me on my mistakes, but I need friends to help me get better. That is the definition of a friend.

Who do you have to hold you accountable? Can you trust that they will tell you the truth whether you want to hear it or not?

Make a list of 3 people that you know will always keep you accountable.

**TAKEAWAY:** If you love me, hold me accountable.

#OGHBYRG

## DAY 266: DREAM VS REALITY

Not having you by my side on yesterday felt like a horrible dream, but the reality is that you were not there.

Not getting your text on what my *"eta"* was for service felt like a dream; but the reality is that you did not send the text.

Not hearing you say after service, "Go get some rest boss man," felt like a dream; but the reality is – is that you didn't tell me that.

I woke up to realize again that it was not a dream, it's reality. All I can say my dude, is that my family and the church family will be by your wife's and kids' sides. They will want for nothing.

Your *"eta"* to heaven seems too soon. Take your rest my dude, and God I thank you for the 33 1/2 years you let lil Murphy be in my life.

Many will say, *"gone too soon,"* but the reality is that we all are, "soon to be gone." The question is, will you be ready?

This was a tough one, I lost one of the closest people to me, Murphy Jamerson Jr.; but I have the greatest church family and support system in the world. We will get through this together. Please keep his wife, children, brothers and sisters, parents and family in fervent prayer.

**TAKEAWAY:** Sometime in life you will wish that your reality was only a dream.

#OGHBYRG

## DAY 267: ONE ACCORD!

When we all come together as one, there is nothing that can come between us or stop us. We are truly stronger together!

I am reminded of a story I read in the Bible on how the Day of Pentecost, everyone was on one accord and a mighty move of God took place!

Then I read another story about a man named Ezekiel who was a prophet, and God took him in a vision and sat him down in a valley full of dry bones. Then God told Ezekiel to prophesy (speak) to the bones, "Hear the word of the Lord." Once Ezekiel did what God commanded, the bones came together, stood on their feet and became a great army!

This all took place because Ezekiel listened, and they were all on one accord!

Whatever confusion or division you may be experiencing, I challenge you to simply get on one accord.

**TAKEAWAY:** Together we stand and divided we do fall.

#OGHBYRG

## DAY 268: GOD IS IN CONTROL.

As much as we want things our way, the reality is that God is in control.

Although God is in control of the result and His will, will be done, He still gives us choice. God will not force you to do anything.

Can you imagine marrying a person that was forced to be with you? Yes, they are with you, but every day you can feel the disconnect because they really do not want to be with you.

I told you the other day that someone near and dear to my heart passed away. I did not understand and it's not for me to. I thanked God for the years he allowed me to have Murphy Jr. in my life because God is in control. There is a good intent behind everything He does, because God is a loving Father.

**TAKEAWAY:** *"Only God can take something from you and comfort you at the same time."* – Pastor Marlon Lock

#OGHBYRG

## DAY 269: REST MY DUDE!

As difficult as it is to lose someone you love, you must find a way to be at peace with it and know that they are resting.

The next time that you go to the cemetery, I want you to look at a head stone. Don't look at the name but look at the dash between the name. The dash is what that person did while on earth.

What will your dash say about you?

**TAKEAWAY:** You fought a good fight, you kept the faith, you finished your course. Now get some rest. Gone but never forgotten. Thank you so much for being you. (my thoughts about Murphy Jamerson Jr.)

#OGHBYRG

## DAY 270: DON'T FOCUS ON THE STORM.

In life we deal with so many weather-related storms; from rain storms to snow storms.

We also deal with life storms. Are you prepared for the storms of life? If prepared, you won't focus on the storm itself, you'll focus on following the guidelines of getting out of the storm.

Remember if you fail to prepare then you are preparing to fail.

Take a few moments to go over areas of your life that you have not prepared for and get prepared. Things such as life insurance, a will, home owners' insurance, and fire protection are all related to preparation.

**TAKEAWAY:** *"The next time it rains don't focus on the rain, focus on opening the umbrella."* – Marlon Lock

#OGHBYRG

## DAY 271: ALL YOU GOT IS YOU.

While in San Antonio at the Final Four, I was with my son and he wanted to walk up this huge flight of stairs. He asked was I going up the stairs with him, I said no you go ahead, and I'll take a picture.

Did I take the picture? Yes, but there was actually a life lesson in having him go up the stairs by himself. I wanted him to know that in life, when you are climbing, everyone cannot go, and everyone won't go. I said son, *"All you got is you."*

I teach my son daily to love God with all his heart, always take care of his mom and sisters and do right by people.

At the end of the day, when it's all said and done – you got you. Take care of you! Everything else will fall into place.

**TAKEAWAY:** My son was born with a lot on his shoulders, but they are broad. With God, he can carry it all.

#OGHBYRG

## DAY 272: SNICKERS REALLY DO SATISFY.

Ok please pay close attention to today's lesson.

I am at the game with my son and I was doing great with my eating regimen. I try to eat every 2 to 3 hours to keep my metabolism burning and not get hungry. I also try to stay away from soda and drink a gallon of water every day.

Well...what happened was, I missed a meal. Please hear me. Never miss a meal!

We are at the game and my son is eating nachos, hot dogs, slushies... and nothing is bothering me, but I know I need to eat something. It was working until....

He opened up his snickers!

When I tell you the caramel hanging, the chocolate falling, and the smell of the peanuts spoke to me. I heard small voices in my head telling me, *"Just eat it. You deserve it. It won't hurt your diet that much."*

Has this ever happened to you? My question is, did you listen to those voices?

Well I sure did, and it was worth it!!!

**TAKEAWAY:** Eat the snickers and be satisfied

#OGHBYRG

## DAY 273: YOU WON'T ALWAYS BE MOTIVATED BUT YOU MUST LEARN TO ALWAYS BE DISCIPLINED!

*"Motivation gets you going but discipline keeps you growing."* – John Maxwell, 15 Invaluable Laws of Growth

**TAKEAWAY:** Don't let the word *"motivation"* trick you.

#OGHBYRG

## DAY 274: TOO MUCH, BUT NOT ENOUGH TIME.

You have too much time to waste time because you don't have enough time.

I've learned that one thing you can never get back is time. So, you must value it and make others value your time as well.

When I first became senior pastor in April of 2009, I tried to be everything for everyone until I realized I was not God. God is the only one that can be everywhere all the time. After setting healthy boundaries and realizing that there is some stuff that I just could not do or be apart of, life became a lot easier to handle.

I still have a heavy schedule, but I include time for myself as well as my family.

Be careful not to fall in the trick bag of thinking you have so much time. With the time you do have – make sure you're not wasting it.

**TAKEAWAY:** You can get so many things back but one thing you can't ever get back is time.

#OGHBYRG

## DAY 275: VOLUNTEER

Volunteer – an unpaid worker; one who enters into or perform(s) of his own free will.

God has blessed our ministry with some incredible volunteers. Many reach out, wanting to do something for the Lord in some shape, form or fashion, just wanting to serve.

If you are a part of any ministry, please find something to do to help it out. Make sure whatever you do, you do so that God can get the glory.

I pray that every servant be strengthened, and unexpected doors are opened for you because of your heart to serve; in Jesus's name, amen.

If you know someone who serves faithfully in whatever capacity, please let them know their value.

**TAKEAWAY:** To all volunteers, your sacrifice has not gone unnoticed.

#OGHBYRG

## DAY 276: WHEN THE SMOKE CLEARS.

Hey family, so many obstacles can and will come in route to your next level.

During those difficult times you will notice how you can feel all alone as if nobody cares or even understands but trust me when I tell you that the smoke is getting ready to clear!

What you did during the smoke, to get through, stay true to yourself.

You were never alone. God just got your attention to become more focused on Him. Just know that it was good to be left feeling alone. It allowed you to grow, mature, trust God, and refocus.

Get ready for your breakthrough. *"When the smoke clears,"* you will see just how bright your future is.

**TAKEAWAY:** Love y'all family and there is nothing that you can do about it.

#OGHBYRG

# DAY 277: GOD IS LOVE.

No matter how low you may get or how far you may stray, remember that God is love.

The Bible says, *"For God so loved the world that he gave his only begotten son, that whosoever believes in him should not perish but have everlasting life."* John 3:16

Then it goes on to say how God sent not his son (Jesus) into the world to condemn it, but to save it.

I think that's so awesome; to have someone's real love is enough, even in our mess! But then not condemn us? Wow, God is love.

**TAKEAWAY:** Take advantage of God's love. It is real.

#OGHBYRG

## DAY 278: FAITH + SUPPORT = WIN!

Faith and belief are often talked about as being the same thing, but they are very different. You can believe that your situation will change but until you put forth the effort and make the change, it'll never be faith, it'll always be belief.

It's cool to support others because one day you will want someone to support you. Trust me, you do not want to be that one that never supports and then all of a sudden need support, because it just may not happen.

**TAKEAWAY:** Go after it and get it. While getting it don't forget to support others along the way. You may just need their support and it's a pretty cool feeling to help someone else.

#OGHBYRG

## DAY 279: UNCOMMON FAVOR FROM AN UNCOMMON PLACE.

I need you to know that this week God is going to do something for you that is going to blow your mind!

Why you ask? Because He is God and He can do what He desires.

Life can make us feel empty and low, but if you walk with expectancy, it is certain to happen.

I want you to expect a door that has been closed, to open. I want you to expect a promotion.

Good vibes and good energy bring about good things because good energy is attractive.

So, expect a favor these next 7 days, from an uncommon place.

**TAKEAWAY:** Please share this with 5 people that you want to experience this as well. Be it unto you in Jesus's name!

#OGHBYRG

## DAY 280: YOU PRAY – LET GOD CHANGE.

It can be difficult wanting someone or something to change and it seems like it's taking forever right?

Well let me help you with this process... Everything is in God's timing. You cannot rush God's time and you cannot slow it down, all you can do is get in rhythm with Him.

Waiting is not the easiest thing, but it is necessary. You still must wait. There is something to be learned during the wait. There is something to be placed into position during the wait. There is something to be moved out of the way, during the wait.

One of my favorite scriptures is Psalms 40. It talks about how when you wait patiently God will respond to your cry.

**TAKEAWAY:** Be encouraged and trust the process. It will work out in your favor.

#OGHBYRG

## DAY 281: YOU WILL ALWAYS BE MY BABY.

At age 18, I had my first child. A beautiful baby girl named Tone'y. I'll admit that it was difficult.

I was only a teenager. Suddenly, I had a load of responsibility. Tone'y didn't come with instructions, a set of rules, and money. She just came and depended on her parents to provide for her.

Her mom and I were both extremely young, but we were dedicated to giving our daughter the best life possible. I cut hair, I cut grass, I washed cars, and did whatever I could legally do to make sure that my baby girl was good.

I had an opportunity to play Division 1 basketball, but I chose to stay home, get a job to support and be involved in my daughter's life. I made a vow that I would be the best dad that I could be, and I am proud to say that's exactly what I did. I did my best!

Now here we are many years later. Tone'y's graduated from college and is living an awesome life. I am married with four other children and Tone'y's the big sister. Man, how time flies but I've truly enjoyed the ride.

Tone'y, I love you and thanks for helping me become a

father. And remember you'll always be my baby girl.

**TAKEAWAY:** You may have made mistakes while young, but just know you will out grow them, and you'll look back and see that it wasn't a mistake at all. It was actually a miracle.

#OGHBYRG

## DAY 282: SOMETIMES YOU HAVE TO LOSE TO WIN.

In life we don't want to lose. Here is a different perspective: It is never a loss when you learn from it.

I am so grateful for all my losses because it helped me to show others how to win. Most people are ashamed of setbacks, not realizing that your setbacks were just a set up for your comeback!

Embrace your struggles! Let people know how far you've come! Your struggle is what made you who you are.

**TAKEAWAY:** The next time you feel like you lost, laugh because you just won.

#OGHBYRG

## BDAY 283: SEED-TIIIIIIIIIME – HARVEST.

I know that you want it so bad and I know that you planted that seed, but please, please, please give it time.

You think you are ready for it, but it is possible that you may not be. You would rather not get it when you want it because you are not ready. If you get it too soon you could mess up and lose it forever. So be patient.

Don't plant the seed and give up on it to soon. Why? Because someone else will reap the harvest. Just hold on and give the seed you planted tiiiiiiiiiiiime!

**TAKEAWAY:** When you keep planting seeds, you'll keep reaping a harvest.

#OGHBYRG

## DAY 284: HAPPY BIRTHDAY

I don't know when your birthday is. If it's today, then what a coincidence right? If not, you'll have one coming up within the next 365 days.

I know birthdays are a big deal. We have a party, receive gifts, and just enjoy being and feeling special on that day. I want to make sure that you know you should feel good every single day of the year; not just one day.

Go ahead and enjoy your birthday – it's yours; Review the good as well as the not so good of the past year and build on it.

Happy birthday (or soon to be) and may you be blessed with many more.

**TAKEAWAY:** Live everyday like it is your birthday.

#OGHBYRG

## DAY 285: THE AUDIENCE OF ONE.

I have ministered to thousands of people and I have sang in stadiums that were sold out.

I have ministered to small audiences and I have sang with just a room full. Each time, I always gave my best no matter who was in the room! I could care less about the size of the crowd because I always sing and minister to the audience of one. That's right. I want God to be pleased in everything I do, and I want my family to be proud. Everything else will take care of itself.

I am challenging you to do the same thing. Do what you do for an audience of one, this will take pressure off you and allow you to focus on what is really important.

**TAKEAWAY:** *"When God is pleased, nobody else matters."* – Marlon Lock

#OGHBYRG

## DAY 286:
## IT'S OKAY TO BE TIRED BUT NOT OKAY TO QUIT.

Going after your goals and dreams in any area of life can sometimes be exhausting!

Almost to the point that you even consider going another route, taking on a new endeavor or even saying, *"Well maybe it's not meant to be."*

Let me encourage your hearts and assure you that it is meant to be, that's why it was placed on your heart to go after it in the first place. Here is what you do: take a break, get restored, take a nap, have a snack, and get back at it!

**TAKEAWAY:** It's okay to get tired but it's not okay to quit.

#OGHBYRG

## DAY 287: IF YOU WANT CHANGE – BE THE CHANGE.

From a child to an adult, people are always talking about change.

Many people talk about the change but don't want to be the change. Change must start from within, but most people try to change from the *"without."* How to do this you ask? Be honest with you! Admit the areas that you struggle in and make those areas better.

You must commit to change first!

**TAKEAWAY:** Your change can start today. Remember effort gets results.

#OGHBYRG

## DAY 288: ENJOY THE RIDE!

My wife started a charity event that gives bikes away to underprivileged children. Not only a bike and helmets, but a Bible as well!

She does this in honor of her mother who passed away, but always allowed my wife to experience the best life possible with the simplest things in life.

We often think we need more money or more time. The reality is you need to be a good steward of the money you do have and prioritize your time.

So, enjoy the ride! You have so much to live for and to be thankful for! Go and be great!

**TAKEAWAY:** Never overlook the small beginnings.

#OGHBYRG

## DAY 289: ALL IS WELL!

I know you may be going through right now and life may seem a little rough but trust me, "all is well!"

I need you to say this out loud and mean it! Why out loud? Because what is in you is waiting to come out. All you must do is let it out!

All is well, and this is the appointed time for you to come forth!

Your dreams will come forth.

Your goals will come forth.

Your family will come forth.

Why? Because all is well!

**TAKEAWAY:** While in your next storm, grab an umbrella and say, *"All is well!"*

#OGHBYRG

## DAY 290: GET A MENTOR.

Find someone that can coach you on this journey called life. I thought for years that I had it all under control and I would just *"figure it out,"* but while trying to *"figure it out,"* I burned out!

It's not that I didn't want better, I just needed a mentor to show me how to get better, how to manage better, how to be better.

My granddad, Eldridge Lock, was the greatest mentor in the world! He was a man of faith and integrity. He mentored me on how to be a better man, son, servant, husband, friend, worker, and so on and so forth. The biggest mentoring lesson I received from my granddad was having faith in God.

I become emotional talking about him because what he poured into my life has changed it forever.

Find someone to mentor you. Ask as many questions as possible and always let them know how much you value their information.

**TAKEAWAY:** Thanks Paw Paw, I thank you so much for what you have instilled in me. I know you are gone but you will never be forgotten because you still live through me.

#OGHBYRG

## DAY 291: STOP TRYING AND DO IT!

Faith must be put into action and, if not careful, we block the very thing we are entitled to because of doubt and fear.

You have a deal that you are supposed to close, a promotion you are supposed to have, a business you should be partnering with, but you don't have it because you are going to "try and see."

While you are *"trying"* someone else is *"getting!"*

I found the word "try" only 4 times in the New Testament section of the Bible, and they both dealt with being tested. I challenge you to stop what you are doing right now and make the call! Send the email! Send the text! Go knock on the door! If you can't get through the door – go through the window!

**TAKEAWAY:** Let's get it! Please share with someone you believe is on the verge of a breakthrough. Contact them now and tell them to go get it!

#OGHBYRG

## DAY 292: HOLD YOUR PEACE.

Long story short, my wife was disrespected at a gas station that we have supported for years. She didn't tell me and told the kids not to tell me because she didn't want me to respond the wrong way. Time goes by and I realize we weren't going to the gas station. One day I pulled in and my daughter Asia said, *"Dad you know we don't go here anymore."* That obviously led to me finding out what happened.

I really was frustrated because I don't like to see my wife, kids or my mother hurt. I feel if I have never hurt them, I am not gonna sit back and allow someone else to do it.

This incident had me extremely heated, and the *"flesh side"* of me wanted to at least have a face-to-face talk with the owner. I am not a tough guy at all (I just watch a lot of movies).

It feels good to handle things the right way. I want to encourage someone to simply *"hold your peace,"* the person(s) trying to get you to react are not even worth the energy.

**TAKEAWAY:** Exodus 14:14, *"The Lord shall fight for you and you shall hold your peace."*

#OGHBYRG

## DAY 293: CONGRATULATIONS!

Sometimes in life you need to hear it before it happens!

Today is that day! You have been working on something and it has been a bit stressful and frustrating at times. Guess what? You're almost there!

I am telling you congratulations in advance. I am letting you know that what you are after, you are about to reach.

Go have a slice of apple pie with a scoop of vanilla ice cream. What's the occasion? It's the pre-party of your accomplishment!

**TAKEAWAY:** Don't wait until the battle is over, shout now!

#OGHBYRG

## DAY 294: CAUGHT OFF GUARD!

Something will happen that will catch you off guard.

You can't let the *"moment"* frustrate you so much that it turns into moments. Notice the added *"s."* I have allowed one bad moment to turn into many and I had to learn from them.

Here is what you do: embrace the caught-off-guard moment and make sure that you learn from it. Be sure to share with others how you felt and what you did to get your normalcy back.

**TAKEAWAY:** Something will catch you off guard, but please don't let it keep you off guard.

#OGHBYRG

## DAY 295: ACCEPT THE CRITICISM.

That's right accept it. Not just the constructive criticism but the hurtful criticism as well.

Here's why. Let it fuel you to your greatness! I don't know about you, but I like when the odds are stacked against me! I like when I have to dig a bit deeper and go a bit harder!

I like when they act like they want to see me succeed but really want me to fail. It's like gasoline to a car.

Stop crying over people talking about you.

Stop complaining that they don't support you.

Stop looking at others to support your dream and you be what you expect others to be. Show them how it is done.

Become undeniably good!

**TAKEAWAY:** Just remain humble. Sometimes we look for support from people when they cannot and do not support themselves. Remember the One person in the audience from day 285.

#OGHBYRG

## DAY 296: GET IN POSITION.

We must learn how to get in position to receive what we have been expecting.

I look at it as being prepared as well. Many times, we are wanting this or that, but the reality is we haven't gotten ourselves in position to get those things.

In the Bible there was a man named Zacchaeus who wanted to see Jesus, but because he was so short, he couldn't see over the crowd. Zacchaeus ran ahead of the crowd and climbed into a tree to see Jesus. While passing by Jesus looked up and said to Zacchaeus, "Come down."

Not only did Jesus call him by his name but also, he went to his home with Zacchaeus.

All of this happened because Zacchaeus got into position.

**TAKEAWAY:** Doors are about to open for you once you get in position.

#OGHBYRG

## DAY 297: I CAN'T FORGET.

Today I want you to remember that person who did something for you that changed and affected your life in such a positive way that you'll never forget it.

It could be a small act of kindness that helped you to remember to always be kind.

It could be a meal that was cooked especially for you with all your favorites.

It could be a teacher that did not give up on you.

It could be a person that served in our military that helped keep us safe.

Whatever it may be just don't forget it. Be sure to let it motivate you to do something for someone that they'll never forget. I'll never forget what the Lord did for me and He's still doing it.

**TAKEAWAY:** Memories last forever.

#OGHBYRG

## DAY 298: A PICTURE IS WORTH A THOUSAND WORDS.

I like looking at pictures. Whether it's in a home or office building, pictures always speak to me.

Pictures tell a story without ever using words. Pictures set the tone of so many events.

Painters are such great communicators because they tell stories with paint and a paint brush. Without any words, we know exactly what they're saying. What pictures do you paint each and everyday? What story are you telling without saying a word?

**TAKEAWAY:** Make sure you live a life so grand that after you're gone, your picture alone will speak volumes.

#OGHBYRG

## DAY 299: NO OPPORTUNITY WASTED!

I want you and need you to take advantage of every opportunity that presents itself to you.

No opportunity is too big or too small.

The small opportunities are preparing you for the big one. Put the work in and the positive energy you need from the beginning. You have been waiting on this moment for a while now. Go get it! Make sure you have a great support system and team in place to assist you.

It could be a seminar, a training, a webinar, a podcast, a 10-minute read of a book, an older gentleman telling stories, etc. You can learn from anyone.

Do not waste the chance to learn. Remember, no opportunity wasted!

**TAKEAWAY:** Remember every opportunity is an opportunity.

#OGHBYRG

# DAY 300: STAY HUNGRY NEVER GREEDY!

Today I want you to appreciate the drive that you have shown as well as the hunger that keeps pushing you. Make sure you never lose that. Hunger and passion will propel you to that next level!

Hunger and passion will cause people to see in you what they don't see in others. Hunger and passion will cause promotions in every aspect of your life from home to work. Any endeavor you are involved in will be better because of you.

As you grow, stay hungry but never become greedy. Greed will cause you to become selfish and not think of others. Greed will cause you to lose your integrity. Greed will cause healthy relationships to become unhealthy.

Remember family, you are blessed to be a blessing! While in pursuit of your goal, make sure that you go about it the right way.

**TAKEAWAY:** Stay humble and never cheat! Always do right by people and right will always, I mean always, come back to you. Stay hungry but never greedy. Love y'all family and ain't nothing you can do about it.

#OGHBYRG

## DAY 301: JESUS SAVES!

Everyone knows my belief in Jesus Christ and how I've dedicated my life to Him.

I do not try to force people to believe what I believe, and I don't fight against what others believe. I love people for who they are and where they are.

However, I would like to share with you why I made Jesus my choice. I was at a super low point in my life (suicidal); it's a long story and you'll get all the details in a forthcoming book. What I can share is that Jesus was there to keep me. His love and comfort let me know that despite what I was dealing with, He was there to help me; not judge, condemn, or make matters worse, but make matters better. And guess what, He did!

If what you're doing is not working and you have no peace, and you know you need to change, try Jesus.

**TAKEAWAY:** I am not sure what you may be dealing with or even why you are dealing with it, but I do know someone that can make it all better… that's right, Jesus! If He can do it for me, I am convinced that He can do it for you.

#OGHBYRG

# DAY 302: MY SQUAD!

When you hear the word squad what comes to mind? For me, I instantly think of teams.

I think of how teams are formed and are called squads. This is the term we used when I was a young man playing basketball at the parks. We would always walk up and say, "What squad is next?"

We would get our 5 guys and go all over taking on the local competition at each park. We would strategize and come up with game plans on who would do what for the team. Each person had a role and was expected to fulfill that role.

Fast forward as a husband, dad, pastor and business owner, I still have my squad. Only now, it's not just for fun. So much more depends on me having the right squad. One critical mistake can not just affect me, but everyone connected with me.

So, I choose my squad/team very carefully and prayerfully. I recommend you do the same.

**TAKEAWAY:** When picking your squad make sure you have people not like you. If you all think the same, you'll never grow.

#OGHBYRG

## DAY 303: FINISH STRONG!

I think that it is important to discuss how we finish anything in life.

I have learned that the energy we start a thing with often times is not the energy we finish with. This is normal for so many people. I believe to be the best that we can be in all areas of our lives we must finish strong.

For example, I tell all employees to make sure they finish out the work week strong. Don't go into Friday already checked out and in weekend mode. Be so focused on Friday that you get some of your Monday work load done. Finish strong!

I tell my children that when they get to the last semester of school to be just as focused as they were at the beginning of the year. Finish strong!

**TAKEAWAY:** It is how you start anything but also how you finish as well, so finish strong!

#OGHBYRG

# DAY 304:
## IF TIRED OF STARTING OVER STOP QUITTING.

The law of consistency says, *"Motivation gets you going but discipline keeps you growing."* – John Maxwell

I was doing an at home workout dvd and the lady said something that slapped me in the face. I was working out but eating bad. I would fall off from doing the workouts and I said, *"I am so tired of starting over."* Fast forward I hear her say, "If you're tired of starting over, stop quitting."

This was such an eye opener. Today I want you to encourage you not to quit. If you never quit, then you'll never have to start over.

Don't:

Quit on your workouts.

Quit on your goals.

Quit on your marriage.

Quit on your hopes and dreams.

Quit on your children.

Quit on your spouse.

Quit on yourself.

*"The greater the sacrifice the greater the reward."* – unknown

**TAKEAWAY:** You know what to do, now simply do it! You got this!

#OGHBYRG

## DAY 305: FAITH DOWN TO THE GROUND!

I wrote a song entitled *"Faith Down to the Ground"* in 2017. Let me share with you how I came up with this title.

I was leaving Atlanta early one Sunday morning headed back to Milwaukee to minister for our 10:30 am service. Normally my wife sits next to me but for whatever reason we were in the same row but across the aisle from each other. We normally would switch seats with someone but this time we didn't (maybe she was frustrated with me). I looked out of the window of the airplane and began to think about the faith that we all have that ride airplanes.

We do not know the pilot. We do not know the staff. We are in thousands of pounds of metal. We are up in the air with no gas station (I'm just saying). It's pretty scary once you think about it. We all have heard of a plane crashing at some point. Still, we have faith that we will be fine.

Then the words came to me: 30,000 feet up in the air. What if we (human race) could take that same faith down to the ground and use it in every area of our lives? What if we could take that same faith and put it in God. In our families. In our communities. What a different world this would be.

**TAKEAWAY:** The next time you get off the plane, take that faith with you.

#OGHBYRG

## DAY 306: STRENGTH

Strength does not come from what you can do. It comes from what you thought you could not do.

Make sure that you don't get it twisted! It is easy to do what you already do; but you must dig a bit deeper and stretch a little further if you really want to achieve your dreams. Ask yourself this question. If it comes that easy, do I really want it that bad?

**TAKEAWAY:** It can and will get rough, but you got this!

#OGHBYRG

## DAY 307: YOU BE THE LIGHT.

We hear it all the time. This is what is wrong with the world today. We need to change this, or we need to fix that.

Then you hear that this school is bad, or these teachers are not teaching. Or you hear I don't like this church and this pastor did or said this. Then it spills over into you not liking your job or the neighborhood you live in.

Can you see this vicious cycle that so many people have created? My suggestion to you today is that you be the light. That's right. It's easy to be a part of the problem, but how about being part of the solution.

**TAKEAWAY:** Complainers will always find something to complain about.

#OGHBYRG

# DAY 308: GIVE BACK.

I told you on a prior day how my wife started an organization on behalf of her mother who passed away unexpectedly. Let me tell you that whenever you give from the heart, you'll always have more than enough. God has a way of blessing people who give, and truly give from the heart.

Every year after we give the bikes away, we have so many bikes left over. So, what do we do? We ride pass parks, playgrounds, barbershops, all over and just pass out the remaining bikes.

The smiles on the faces of the parents and children are priceless!

I challenge you to find some organization or some family or some individual to give back to.

**TAKEAWAY:** *"Remember that the sower always has seed."* – Marlon Lock

#OGHBYRG

## DAY 309: DADDY DAUGHTER DANCE!

Ok, so I am not a dancer. I am really not a dancer. I don't think you get it. Nothing about me is set up to dance! But somehow, I ended up signing up for a daddy daughter dance at her dance school's winter dance recital.

My Sydney was so excited, and we took lessons every week to prepare for this big dance recital.

I was leary about it but then I heard a song on the radio called, *"Dance with My Father Again,"* by Luther Vandross.

This song touched me like never before. I began to think of the loss of my dad and how I would love to be able to sing, dance, talk, whatever it may be, with him again. It motivated me to practice and practice and practice to be the best dad out on the stage with my Sydney.

Well I nailed it and Sydney was the best partner and trainer a dad could ever have.

**TAKEAWAY:** Sydney will always remember that she got a chance to dance with her dad.

#OGHBYRG

## DAY 310: HAPPY FATHERS' DAY!

To all the dads, being a parent is not the easiest thing in the world. To be quite honest, it's pretty scary.

You get no instructions and no test run. It's just, *"Hey I am pregnant, and you are the father."* Then the baby comes. You are so proud, and you have so many expectations, and then life hits!

It is easy to get off track or come up short. If not careful, we just give up on our responsibilities and who suffers, the child.

I just want to encourage some dad today that may be looking for an instruction manual... I use the Bible. It has helped me in every area in life and it will do the same for you.

Pick your head up and go love on your child. He or she is waiting.

To the dads that are holding it down and being the best dad you can be, please know that your sacrifice has not gone unnoticed. Way to be a light to others. They are watching, and your children will always know that you were there.

**TAKEAWAY:** Having a baby doesn't make you a father. There's a responsibility that goes along with it.

#OGHBYRG

# DAY 311: ALL BY MYSELF!

These are three words that most people do not want to hear; but these three words are where the magic happens. That's right, all by myself.

It is easy to be motivated by others, but the reality is that you have to have a game plan when you are all by yourself. By yourself is where you get mentally tough. It is where you learn that all you have is you and only you.

The moment you depend on others is the moment others let you down. Appreciate others but just know at the end of the day all you got is you. Put the hours in by yourself. Get the reps in by yourself. Read the book by yourself. Take another class by yourself. Go to church by yourself. Once you get it for yourself then you can help someone else.

**TAKEAWAY:** *"It's what you do alone that shows up in the crowd."* – Marlon Lock

#OGHBYRG

## DAY 312:
## PMA

Positive mental attitude!

I gave you three words on yesterday, well here's another three. Positive mental attitude.

Remember that it is never the situation that is really the issue. It's all in how you respond to it.

You must have the right attitude.

Your attitude starts the moment you wake up and what you tell yourself or what you let enter your ear gate (what you hear).

When I get up, I pray and then read my Bible or some type of growth and development book. This gets me going! I heard Les Brown say that the first 20 minutes after you wake up are the most important of your day.

Every day that I wake up, the fact that I woke up gives me joy! It assures me that I have another day to give God praise. Another day to see my wife and children. Another day to be a light to a dark world. Another day to right my wrongs. Wow! Just look at how a positive mental attitude can change your life!

Be careful not to let *"negative"* people, situations, etc., sap your PMA. Everyday we can find a reason to complain and be frustrated but in that same moment you can choose to be positive.

**TAKEAWAY:** I have heard that misery loves company and that may be true, but I also know that misery needs to be told that it is not welcomed. Why? Because I choose to have a PMA. So please, make the choice to have a positive mental attitude. Trust me, it makes life so beautiful.

#OGHBYRG

## DAY 313: EVERYONE MAKES MISTAKES.

In life we all at some point will make some mistakes, and some mistakes will cost you more than others...

Please don't let a mistake stop you from moving forward. I've made so many mistakes in my life, but for each one of them I learned something. I took them as life lessons to help others not go through what I have gone through.

I used to hear as a child that experience is the best teacher. As I have grown older, I feel that other people's experiences are the best teacher. Some things you don't have to go through.

I have such a heart for those who have fallen. Probably because I fell myself so many times. I don't want you to look at how many times you have fallen but look at how many times you have gotten back up!

**TAKEAWAY:** Don't look down on a man unless you're picking him up.

#OGHBYRG

## DAY 314: I LOVE MY MOMMA.

I just wanted to share with everyone (again) the love that I have for my mother. When I tell you this is one of, if not the, strongest women that I know, please believe me.

My mother raised my brothers and I the best that she could. She raised us as God-fearing young men. My dad was incarcerated when I was a child, and when I was 11, he died of a heroin overdose. I am not ashamed of that, it's just what happened. My mom stepped up and gave my brothers and I the best life possible. My mom had a way of making struggling fun. As poor as we were, from getting assistance from the government to wearing hand me downs, my mom made it seem like we were rich. It wasn't until I got older that I realized how awesome my mom really was.

God truly blessed my brothers and I with the greatest mother in the world.

**TAKEAWAY:** To those who have lost a mother or someone who was like a mother to you, just know that her love is still with you. To those that still have their mother, spoil her and love her as much as you can. There's nothing like a mother.

#OGHBYRG

## DAY 315: GATHER AROUND THE TABLE.

I think sitting around the table with loved ones, friends, colleagues, etc... is so important.

It allows you to not just connect but build a bond that can last for a lifetime. Think about all the great moments and conversations that happen around the table. Think about the holidays when we sit, eat and tell stories.

For me, in the church settings this happens quite often. I am so excited to be in partnership with incredible ministers of the gospel! To sit among believers that all have the same mindset and purpose to reach out and save a dying world means so much!!!

I cannot wait to see the lives that will be impacted by the lives we touch! I am asking God to strengthen all ministries and all pastors all over this nation in Jesus's name! Amen!

**TAKEAWAY:** Take full advantage whenever you gather around the table to eat.

#OGHBYRG

# DAY 316: PUT OUT THE FIRE!

One day members of a fire house in our area gave a demonstration at our church's picnic of how fire trucks and the equipment work. The kids as well as the adults were in awe!

To see everything that they must know and how high the ladder extends was impressive. You know, it is different seeing it from the perspective of a child and then again as an adult.

While looking at the demonstration I thought about this: whenever there is a fire and the fire truck comes, it is in position to put the fire out! Think about that.

No matter how big or small the fire truck puts out the fire.

So many times, we go around with things in our heart and before you know it, it builds and builds, and everything is destroyed... not realizing that all you had to do was put out the fire!

Make a committed effort to put out the fire. What is *"burning up,"* should be *"blessing up."* Be sure to put the fire out!

**TAKEAWAY:** Are you a fire starter or a fire extinguisher?

#OGHBYRG

# DAY 317: DON'T GIVE THE REACTION THEY WANT.

You have been on this journey with me for 317 days. Let me just congratulate you now because you will make it through all 365 days. You have come too far to turn around now.

Everyone may not be happy for you. Some may feel that this means nothing and is worthless. That is just how it goes. You can be the sweetest, most loyal person in the world, and somebody will try to pull you down and disrupt your peace. Always remember: Misery loves company and the only way a miserable person can "think" they feel better is by trying to tear someone else down.

Shaking my head... the next time someone says something to make you feel bad, simply say, *"thank you"* and smile. Always remember, never give the reaction they want. I love when people say and do things to frustrate me, the look on their face when I say thank you... It's priceless.

**TAKEAWAY:** When someone shows you who they are... Believe them!

#OGHBYRG

## DAY 318:
## I DON'T BELIEVE HE BROUGHT ME THIS FAR TO LEAVE ME.

I must let the preacher come out. You probably don't know a whole lot about my life other than what I have shared. This book came about from my daily thoughts and endeavors. So, you get me from many different angles (if you will).

My future book will really give you more intimate details of my struggles and how I overcame them. But I will say this, in my lowest moments in life I often found myself talking to God saying, "God I don't believe you brought me this far to leave me." Every single time he assured me that he was still there.

I just want to encourage you today that you did not make it this far to be left alone. You may feel alone but you are not alone. No one may be physically around, but someone is there. You may have fallen but you are being picked up even now. You may not know it, but God brought you this far. That's right! Even if you do not confess God, it was still God that brought you up to this point. Keep your head up. This is only a test to go with your testimony.

**TAKEAWAY:** When I should have died, I didn't. So why not live life to the fullest!

#OGHBYRG

## DAY 319: LOOK UP ABOVE (GOD SEES YOU)!

While going through a storm or any difficult situation, it is so easy to panic or fret when all we have to do is stop and look up above.

That's right, above is where our help comes from. Psalms 121 says, "I will lift up mine eyes unto the hills from whence cometh my help. My help comes from the Lord..."

How cool is it to know that whatever I am going through I can just look up for my help.

Don't look down in despair, look up.

Don't look around at others, look up.

All your help is in your looking up.

Please share this with someone to let them know that God has everything under control.

**TAKEAWAY:** Look up in the sky. It's a bird, no it's a plane. No, it's your help!

#OGHBYRG

# DAY 320: DO YOU KNOW?

Listen! Your competition is working right now.

The same thing that you want to be great at, someone right now is going harder than you are! The same deal that you want to get, they want it just as bad. The difference in the results is the person that wants it the most!

Stop making excuses and put the work in!

In writing, studying, dancing, practicing an instrument, working on your game, getting in your word to be a better speaker, going to trainings and conferences... do whatever it takes.

Once you arrive, they will know.

**TAKEAWAY:** You know if you are truly putting the work in.

#OGHBYRG

## DAY 321: MIRACLES STILL HAPPEN.

With all the not so good things that go on in society we can easily become discouraged and frustrated, feeling that life is a drag.

With so much negativity in the world you must look for the positive. Not only look for the positive but surround yourself with positive people. I have learned that in the right environment you can witness miracles. Yes, that's right, miracles! Miracles still happen!

I am reminded of a woman in the Bible who had a blood issue that she dealt with for 12 years. She tried every doctor and spent all her monies on medicines but to no avail. She could not find a cure for her condition. Can you imagine bleeding non-stop for 12 long years?

She decided to touch the hem of Jesus's garment and said, "If I touch the hem of his garment I'll be made whole." Guess what happened? She touched His garment and the blood issue dried up! Now that's a miracle!

You may be thinking, *"Well that was back then."* It was back then and still is today. You are that miracle! Think about what you have been through. Think about the storms you have overcome. Think about the blood issue – the issue that happened in your family and how you overcame. Think about how you pressed your way and kept fighting and how far you've come. Now I know you still have some work to do, but what you have done so far counts as a miracle.

The next time you see someone going through and losing hope, tell them miracles still happen.

**TAKEAWAY:** If you want to see a miracle, just look at me.

#OGHBYRG

## DAY 322: BRIDGE THE GAPS.

Hey! We don't have a lot of time to get from where we are to where we want to be!

What are you doing to bridge those gaps?

In the book, The 15 Invaluable Laws of Growth, John Maxwell talks about 8 different gaps that many people face. I studied these gaps and adjusted my life accordingly, and my life changed forever. Let me share them with you and hopefully you get help as well.

The assumption gap – I assume that I will automatically grow.

The knowledge gap – I don't know how to grow.

The timing gap – it's not the right time to begin.

The mistake gap – I am afraid of making mistakes.

The perfection gap – I must find the best way before I start.

The inspiration gap – I don't feel like doing it.

The comparison gap – others are better than I am.

The expectation gap – I thought it would be easier than this.

Thanks John!

Refocus and recommit to your spiritual goals as well as

carnal (earthly) goals. You got this.

**TAKEAWAY:** Go get the book, The 15 Invaluable Laws of Growth, by John Maxwell

#OGHBYRG

## DAY 323: BE RESOURCEFUL!

I have found that people who are unaccomplished attribute it to, *"lack of resources,"* but on the other hand successful people contribute their success to the, *"abundance of resources."* That's pretty interesting, don't you think?

The reality is, nothing is going to just fall into your lap. You must prepare yourself for what you are expecting. If success came easy, then everyone would be successful. Success takes hard work, commitment and dedication. It takes a sense of urgency and focus like never before.

The resources are all around us, now go be resourceful.

**TAKEAWAY:** You have the same opportunities and the same 24 hours in a day like the next person. No more excuses... Be resourceful – you got this!

#OGHBYRG

## DAY 324: LAUGH!

This may seem like something simple to do but to many it is not. I have heard that laughter is good for the soul. I personally believe that. I find something everyday to laugh about.

Ok, quick story. My wife and I hang out every Monday, just the two of us. This is just a way we make sure each week we are spending quality time with one another. Well on a particular Monday, we were over in Illinois, inside a parking structure. Traffic comes from both ways, so it is important that you drive safe and use your horns because the vehicle from the other direction may or may not see you. I said to my wife, *"Hey boo make sure you blow the horn to alert oncoming traffic."* She replies, "I got this."

After that, someone was coming around really fast, not using the mirrors and almost hit us. Not funny at all, but here is where it gets super funny. I simply let down my window and put my head out of the window and made horn sounds until we got out of the parking structure. I also recorded the entire thing. People were looking at me like I was insane, and my wife could not stop laughing! "argh arghhhhhhh"

We still go back and watch the recorded message on Instagram and laugh just as hard now as when we first did it.

Find something that makes you laugh everyday. There are so many things to complain about so instead find something to laugh about.

**TAKEAWAY:** Laughter is good for the soul.

#OGHBYRG

## DAY 325: GET IN WHERE YOU FIT IN.

Each year I do a walk/run on the behalf of my independent Gospel music label. It's only 1 mile and all the proceeds go to a non-profit organization or charity that has a great cause.

We have supported sickle cell awareness, troubled teens, and the Boys and Girls Club of Greater Milwaukee to name a few.

I do this not only to give back but also to help people make small steps towards fitness goals. You can walk or run and it's only 4 times around the track. So many people are motivated and encouraged because it's doable.

I want to encourage you to support some organization that is doing positive things as well as make sure you are reaching your fitness goals.

Reach out to a friend. Get an accountability partner and go for it. You got this, and you'll feel great helping others as well as yourself.

**TAKEAWAY:** Go get in where you fit in.

#OGHBYRG

## DAY 326: GO GET IT!!!!

You have prayed for it!

You have trained for it!

You have worked for it!

Now go get it!

That's right! Think about what you have been praying for. It is closer than you think.

Think about what you have trained for; the hours you have put in making sure you are ready.

Think about how you have worked your butt off and the blood, sweat, tears and skin you have put in the game.

You think I am going to let you quit? You think your team is going to let you give up now?

This is day 326. You have come too far to turn around now. Get up today and go get it!

**TAKEAWAY:** It's that simple.

#OGHBYRG

## DAY 327: THE SIMPLE THINGS.

What a phrase. The simple things. It is so simple that we tend to overlook it.

In a world where everything and everyone can be so complex, it is good to be able to sit back, slow down and enjoy the simple things.

One summer my family and I were on Sanibel Island. We had so much from. From trying new foods and doing new adventures, it was awesome!

One of the days we wanted to go bike riding. I picked a bike that we all could sit on as a family and we all had to pedal and work together to move on this bike. Boy did we struggle. I mean we really struggled but it was so much fun. It was something really simple that we all will remember for a lifetime.

Slow down today and enjoy the simple things.

**TAKEAWAY:** A walk in the park. A game of tag or cans. Allowing your child to read a book to you. These are the simple things.

#OGHBYRG

## DAY 328: JUST BE YOU!

It's so easy to compare yourself to others, not realizing that this is so unfair to you!

Listen here!

You are incredible

You are amazing

You are pretty

You are handsome

You are smart

You are fearfully and wonderfully made

And... You are next in line for the biggest breakthrough in your life. It's going to come by being you!

Just be you.

**TAKEAWAY:** Nobody is better at being you than you.

#OGHBYRG

## DAY 329: CELEBRATE OTHERS!

One of the greatest things that I have learned in leadership is that you cannot get very far or be an effective leader without others.

When I first began on this quest to be a better leader, I learned quickly that people that say, *"It's lonely at the top,"* were not very good leaders. Why? Because they were unable to bring others with them.

I have had so many mentors in my life that it made me realize the work and effort it takes to raise other leaders. As a leader, when you celebrate your team, they will always go to bat for you and have your back.

Now don't just celebrate to make them feel good, but truly recognize them for the value that they add to you.

I won't get into names because there are way too many to even remember, but I just want to take a moment to thank and celebrate all those that have played any type of role in my life. Small or great, good or bad, it all helped me grow and develop into the man I am today. Without you there would be no me. So, thank you. I celebrate you.

**TAKEAWAY:** Find someone to celebrate every day.

#OGHBYRG

# DAY 330: IT'S TIME!

I've been wanting my son to like basketball since he came out the womb.

He liked... Dinosaurs, Spider-man, Incredible Hulk, Temple Run, Madea, video games, etc....

I was getting nervous because I am like, *"Dude better like basketball."* I never forced it and just let him develop into the young man he wanted to be. I was just willing to be present in his life!

The time came where he wanted to play basketball. All on his own.

I encourage every parent to be present in your child's life. Whatever they dream about and desire to do, you be there to support and make it happen for them. When it's time, not only will you know but they will know.

**TAKEAWAY:** *"To everything there is a season and a purpose."* – Ecclesiastes 3:1

#OGHBYRG

# DAY 331: I AM NOT FALLING!

You got people that want to see you fail, for whatever reason.

They hope that you go back to your former self, because the old you made them feel worth something. But I want you to tell yourself, *"I am not falling!"*

God has brought you from too much and from too far! Go be great and let the devil know... I am not falling!

Every year we take a group of young men between the ages of 10-18 camping. It's a 3-day event. The main purpose is to build them up and teach them certain things that they will need to know to be productive men in society.

One year our theme was: *"I am not falling."* Every obstacle course was set up to really challenge these young men, but they had the entire group yelling at them saying, *"You will not fall!"* It was so awesome! This motivated the one doing the challenge or obstacle course to know and hear that he had a group of people willing to push him, support him, and help him not fall.

Guess what? You have that same group of people pushing you! That's right. There are others reading this book and have committed to each day becoming better than they were the day before. All around the world you have someone believing in you and praying for you that you make it through your 365-day journey.

Let me remind you, that no matter how hard life may seem to appear and no matter what is thrown in your direction. You will not fall!

**TAKEAWAY:** Say out loud, *"I am not falling!"*

#OGHBYRG

# DAY 332: IT'S HOW YOU RESPOND.

This was a rough one for me, but I made it through.

I was at a well-known store that I've been a customer of since a child. I went to this store one day and they had a 30% off sale. I was excited because with 5 children sales are very important.

I am getting my items and my hands are both full to the max. I can't carry anything else and I was not done shopping. I asked an employee could I leave my items at the front register while I finish shopping. He says, *"Just a moment let me check."* I am like, *"well okay,"* still holding all these items. The gentleman says, "We can't hold items up front." I said, *"Why not?"* He said, *"Talk to my manager."* The manager comes out and says the same thing as the worker with no explanation. At this point I am frustrated! Can I be really transparent? I was pissed!

So many thoughts ran through my head. I calmed down and then went and put all my items on a chair and began to walk towards the exit. Different people that saw what was happening began to say it was racial because I am African American, and these individuals were Caucasian.

I simply said, "If that's the case, they will have to pay for it, I cannot let it bother me." I left the store but a young man with me complained and spoke up about it, ultimately giving my telephone number to corporate and they called me.

It took everything in me not to raise a fuss about it. I simply told corporate that I was treated unfairly and choose not to spend money with them. They wanted to offer me a lot of different things, but I declined them all. I did not want anything but what I had originally selected.

I am sharing this with you because so many times we are concerned about what is going on with us that may not be right, but it's how you respond to it that makes the situation better or worse.

**TAKEAWAY:** The next time you have a chance to respond to a not so good situation, voice your opinion but respond with class and dignity. Remember they will need you before you need them.

#OGHBYRG

## DAY 333:
## I AM GRATEFUL.

What is the meaning of grateful? It is feeling or showing an appreciation of kindest; thankful.

I want to take some time to let everyone know how grateful I am for every storm and set back in my life.

I was not happy that I had to go through them, nor did I want to go through, but when I look back everything that I have endured made me who I am today.

Each storm you go through is making you stronger and teaching you humility at the same time. Each lesson given to us in life should be a lesson learned. I am not sure what storms or challenges you have faced or are facing right now but just know be grateful that it's only temporary and it will make you stronger.

Today, I speak a blessing over your life. Your storm is over.

**TAKEAWAY:** Instead of complaining about the storm, be a storm chaser.

#OGHBYRG

## DAY 334: EFFORT GETS RESULTS.

Growing up, I played basketball a lot. It was fun for me on every level.

I have played on really good teams that have won championships as well as really bad teams that didn't have a chance of winning at all, but I truly enjoyed each and every experience.

I had a coach say something to me that has stuck with me for life. He said, *"Effort gets results!"* I mean he screamed it at the entire team. He was letting us know that if we wanted the results of a good team, we had to put forth the effort; not some of the time but all the time. Our coach expressed how he was never the best player, but he felt that nobody could out hustle him. If it was a loose ball, he would get it. If it was a rebound, he would box out hard. Whatever effort play he could make he knew that it would increase his team's chances at winning.

I am asking you to take a good look in the mirror and ask yourself if you are giving your best effort? Are you being the best that you can be to make the people you are connected with better?

If not, why not? Effort gets results in every aspect in life.

Want to be a better spouse? Put forth the effort.

Want to be a better worker? Put forth the effort.

Want to be a better owner? Put forth the effort.

Want to be better at math? Put forth the effort.

You can be the best at whatever it is you put your mind to if you put forth the effort. Now go be great!

**TAKEAWAY:** Let it be your effort!

#OGHBYRG

## DAY 335: GET BACK TO THE FUNDAMENTALS.

One day I was teaching my children some things about the game of basketball. They said they wanted to learn how to play but when I went outside to check on them it was pretty bad. I mean really bad. They did everything wrong.

From dribbling, to passing, to running without dribbling, to pushing and grabbing the other person, I mean it was the worst. I then told them, *"I'll teach you how to play."* They were all excited until I put the basketball up and told them to do line drills.

They were confused and began to complain. They said, *"Why are we running and not playing basketball dad?"* I said we will bring out the basketball shortly but this running you're doing is to let you see what will happen if you don't pay attention to the fundamentals of the game.

When I give you instructions on the basics or fundamentals, I need you to pay attention.

I expressed to them how the game of basketball is the greatest game in the world to me but if you don't learn the fundamentals from the start it won't be fun at all.

My question to you is, do you need to get back to the fundamentals? Not in basketball but in life. It's so easy to get off track – trying all the new, easy ways of doing things, but trust me getting back to the basics works every time.

**TAKEAWAY:** We make *"it"* way harder than what it needs to be. Instead of making things so complicated, get back to the *"fundamentals."*

*"The foundation that was laid for you is what is going to elevate you."* – Marlon Lock

## DAY 336: DOORS ARE OPENING.

In the Bible it talks about how life and death are in the power of the tongue (Proverbs 18:21).

This verse is basically saying that we have to be careful of what we allow to come out of our mouths. You can either speak blessings or cursings over your life. This scripture changed my entire outlook on life.

Today I decided to speak a blessing over your life. I am speaking that doors are opening up just for you! The economy may be bad, but it'll be prosperous for you. Your company may be laying off, but they will give you a promotion. A disease has been running in your family, but it will stop once it gets to you. Because of you, life and peace will be the legacy of your family. That's right, and it's all because doors are opening!

All I need you to do is receive it! In Jesus's name! Don't just believe it but have faith in it. Belief is belief, but faith is putting what you believe in action.

**TAKEAWAY:** If you believe that doors are opening for you or someone you've been praying for please share this!

#OGHBYRG

## DAY 337: WE ALL PLAY A PART.

I partnered with the City of Milwaukee in an effort to bring hope and restoration to our city.

I saw the danger my city was in and knew that if we did not do something about it – and show some concern nobody else would. Prayer is wonderful, and we should pray – but after you pray, and get off your knees, what are you going to do? I just wanted to do my part.

I called out for all people of influence. Our aldermen, barbershop owners, teachers, pastors, street dudes, business owners, coaches, etc… I asked them to come out and support our city and show the world that we are stronger together!

I challenge you to do the same thing. If your city needs to get better, make sure you are doing your part to make it better. It all starts with one. That's right, one person can reach the masses. *"Don't despise small beginnings."* We each play a part. What part are you willing to play?

**TAKEAWAY:** *"I am not asking you to do what you cannot. I am simply asking you to do what you can."* – Marlon Lock

#OGHBYRG

## DAY 338: THANK YOU.

I told you on yesterday how my church family and I partnered with the Milwaukee Police Department in an effort to help drop the crime rate. Here's a letter that I posted on my social media page. It says:

Hey family,

I would just like to say thank you to those who prayed with us, those that prayed for us and those who came out with us.

I had no idea what would happen on yesterday. I did not know anything about media coverage and if anyone would show up at all. I did as I was led.

News may not have shown us walking and praying for the neighborhood. News may not have shown us singing songs of thanksgiving. News may not have shown us loving on the people who came out of their homes. But we didn't do it for the news coverage.

Our intent was to go into the community, pray with the community, strengthen the people in the community and pray for the officers.

A woman gave her life to Christ while we were there and for that reason alone, it was worth it. If we all do what we can, work together, and not condemn one another but support, maybe, just maybe we could be better.

There will always be backlash and negative opinions about what you do. If we did nothing, someone would complain. If we did something, someone would complain. As long as God gets the glory, nothing else matters.

**TAKEAWAY:** *"As long as God gets the glory nothing else matters."* – Kimberly Lock

#OGHBYRG

## DAY 339: WE STILL FIND JOY.

Let me celebrate you out the gate. Why? You might ask. Well let me explain.

Just pause for just a moment and look at everything that you have been through. What would have made most people quit, you did not allow it to stop you. You still found joy in the midst of it all.

It so important that you do not allow the world to take away your joy.

You were born to win!

You lost the job.

You lost the car.

You lost loved ones.

You lost friends.

You were overlooked.

You were not even considered.

But you still found joy in the midst of it all. So today, pat yourself on the shoulder. Go do something good for yourself.

**TAKEAWAY:** You always somehow beat the odds.

*"You're not lucky you're loved."* – Jonathan McReynolds

#OGHBYRG

## DAY 340: DO IT THE RIGHT WAY AND STAY CONSISTENT.

One day, Sydney was struggling with basketball and Bro bro (my son) was making shots.

Sydney says, *"I'll just throw underhand."* I told her, *"No, do it the right way."* Frustrated, still missing the shot, she kept doing it the right way. Doing things the right way will not always seem to be working and taking short cuts like others may seem to be okay, but guess what? It is not ok!

You have too much to lose to take short cuts and become inconsistent.

**TAKEAWAY:** *"What good is having a belly if there's no fire in it? Wake up, drink your passion, light a match and get to work!"* – Simon Sinek, Together is Better

#OGHBYRG

# DAY 341: FAITH VS BELIEF

Let's dive right into this one. Many people believe that faith and belief are one in the same, but they are very different. Let me explain.

Belief is I feel that I can do something. Faith is actually doing it. I am challenging you again today, or should I say I am stretching you, to step out on what you believe in.

I know it may seem a bit uncomfortable to just go for it but what do you have to lose? Nothing. What do you have to gain? Everything! Belief is good, and we need to believe, but activate your belief with your faith.

**TAKEAWAY:** *"Now faith is the substance of things hoped for, the evidence of things not seen."* – Hebrews 11:1 KJV

#OGHBYRG

DAY BY DAY WITH LIFE COACH MARLON LOCK

## DAY 342:
## CALLING ALL SINGLES.

Being single can be one of the most difficult times in life for some and the best time for others. I have been both and I learned so much from both.

First of all, take the time to enjoy your season of being single. Be sure to travel, splurge and take advantage of the fact that you have nobody to answer to but God. Marriage actually starts while single. Here's how.

Start now, while single, learning how to budget and be selfless. Learn now how to share and communicate well. Learn now how to agree to disagree because these are all things as well as other stuff that you will have to know. Most importantly know yourself.

Another thing: Don't put unnecessary pressure on yourself to find your mate. Let it happen organically. Don't say, *"I am getting old or my window is closing,"* just enjoy your season of singleness.

I have learned that a single person can be just as powerful if not more powerful than a couple.

**TAKEAWAY:** Enjoy your single season and listen for the wedding bells that are ringing in your direction.

#OGHBYRG

## DAY 343: FROM THIS TO THAT.

Day 343. Wow look how far we have come. Only 22 days left, and you will have completed one full year with me and the OGHBYRG team.

On our journey together, we have had ups and downs, trials and tribulations, and heartaches and pain. But we made it!

I want you to understand that you had to get through your this to get to your that.

Your this was all the things that were trying to hinder you. It was all the things that made you want to quit. All the obstacles that made you want to give up. Can I tell you what kept you moving forward? It was your that.

Your that (your goals) were greater than your this (your problems). That is why you never gave up. That is why you worked the extra hours. That is why you went back to school. That is why you practiced delayed gratification. That is why you rededicated your life back to God. That is why you mended the relationship back with your family. All because of your that.

Your this almost made you quit, but your that kept you going in the right direction.

**TAKEAWAY:** Thank God for your this and give him praise for your that. You are winning!

#OGHBYRG

#  DAY 344: FAMILY!

This is a subject that is near and dear to my heart. I think family is one of the most important things in the world!

When you think about family this is where it all begins. We did not have a choice in the family we would be born into. We just showed up and had to play with the hand we were dealt.

All families have problems but it's still your family. Families love each other. Some fight each other. Some families don't talk at all. But guess what? They are still family. Take the time to know who your family is and learn as much as you can about them. Some of your older family members have been through things that you may have to go through one day. Why not sit down and spend time with them to get wisdom and knowledge that only comes from time and experience?

Get to know the younger generation and what they have to offer. We all need each other in every family in the world.

Now as you know, I am very transparent. My immediate family is extremely close but over the years my overall family has become very, very distant for many reasons. Regardless of the reasons, I pray that one day my entire family will truly love one another the way a family should. I am looking forward to this day. It will come to pass. Once a family member is gone, they are gone forever.

**TAKEAWAY:** A relationship takes effort from both sides. Don't worry about the other side just make sure your side is up to par.

#OGHBYRG

# DAY 345: PASTOR AND WIFE APPRECIATION.

How did we get here?

So, not sure if you knew this or not but not only am I a life coach, a musician, a husband and a dad, and a former police officer, but I am a full-time pastor. This is what God chose me to do.

I preach the good news of Jesus Christ to those that are lost in sin and I am a light to those in darkness in hopes that they would give their lives to God.

I don't force anyone to believe in my beliefs or do things the way that I do them, but I do share with anyone I come in contact with that Jesus came, suffered, died and rose again so that we all could be saved. I just want to be clear before I proceed.

As a young minister, I never, I mean never dreamed of pastoring. I loved singing and ministering a few times out of the year but never desired to pastor. My wife has her master's degree and was climbing the corporate ladder. I was a police officer for the City of Milwaukee when all of a sudden, our lives changed!

I went from no job, to cutting grass and cutting hair on the side, to working at a company called Master Lock, to back in school, to playing college basketball, to being married, to being divorced, to being married again, to becoming a cop, to then an assistant pastor to the senior pastor, to now having an appreciation service every year in honor of my wife and I.

You gotta be kidding me!

Words cannot express how grateful I am and how humbling this experience is every year. To my church family and my community and to all those that I serve, thanks for appreciating me but without you there would be no me. From the bottom of my heart, thanks and just know that I appreciate all of you!

**TAKEAWAY:** *"Success always takes help."* – Simon Sinek, Together is Better

#OGHBYRG

# DAY 346: YOUR FAITH IS UNDER ATTACK!

If we cannot please God without faith (Hebrews 11:6), then what do you think the devil is going to go after?

I need you to understand this more than anything else. The enemy does not want your things. He does not want your family. He does not want your finances. The enemy only wants your faith. Everything is connected to your faith.

If we cannot please God without faith, then this is what the devil is going to attack.

The enemy will bring all type of distractions your way, all in an effort to make you lose faith in God.

I love in the Bible where it says, *"No weapon formed against you shall be able to prosper."* – Isaiah 54:17. This simply means that the weapon will form (you will see it), but it will not prosper (it will not have power over you).

Be encouraged and just know that the attack is against your faith.

**TAKEAWAY:** When opposition fights you, fight back!

#OGHBYRG

## DAY 347: AUGUST 8, 2018

This is a day I'll never forget as long as I live. It's so much to say, but I'll make it brief.

I leave the gym from playing basketball and I have a cold. A friend of mine tells me to go to urgent care and just get some antibiotics.

I would normally just take some Nyquil and sleep it off, but I had an event that I needed to be my best at coming up in a few days. I went to the doctor, and they were doing the normal "check-in" procedures and asking questions about me and what I did for a living and what brought me in today. You know things like that.

After taking my weight and blood pressure the doctor came in moments later saying, *"An angel brought me in today."* I was like, *"Oh really, what makes you say that?"* He proceeded to tell me that my heart was beating abnormal and that I possibly was having or had a heart attack.

Stop the doggone press! What the what?

I have never been to the hospital, I work out 5 times a week minimum, and I practice clean eating. There's no way this could be happening. They put an IV in me and called the paramedics. They rushed me, red lights and sirens, to the hospital and kept me over night.

So many thoughts came in my head but the main thing I thought about was my wife, kids, and church family. All I kept saying was, *"I didn't have a heart attack and there's nothing wrong with my heart!"* I was adamant about it and would not be persuaded differently. Long story short, test after test after test and being poked more times with needles than a porcupine, I had to take a stress test for them to look at my heart while on a treadmill. They said this would determine the strength of my heart.

After 20 minutes on the treadmill they asked me was I tired yet. I looked at the doctor and said, *"The only thing I am tired of is this hospital."* They had me get off the treadmill and all tests came back negative!

No heart attack!

No heart issues!

No nothing!

That day gave me a new perspective on life. It showed me how in a matter of seconds your life can change forever! I am grateful for the experience because it increased my faith, but it also made me focus on what is really important.

I let go of some things that financially were good but were pulling on me way too much. All is well. Thank you, Jesus!

**TAKEAWAY:** Sometimes you may have to lose in order to truly win. And you actually never lose, you learn.

#OGHBYRG

# DAY 348: PURPOSE BEHIND THE PAIN.

What is purpose? It is the reason for which something is done or created or for which something exists.

I want you to know that there is always a purpose behind your pain! You may not understand it. It may not seem fair, but just know there is a purpose behind it. I have looked back over my life at every storm I have gone through. As painful as they were, there was always a purpose behind the pain.

I realize in pastoring that if I had not been through anything then how could I help someone else get through? You see, that alone gave purpose to my pain, to help someone get through theirs.

The Bible says in Romans 8:28, *"And we know that all things work together for good to them that love God, to them who are the called according to his purposes."*

Stop stressing. There's a purpose behind your pain.

**TAKEAWAY:** *"If it doesn't kill you it can only make you stronger."* – Kanye West

#OGHBYRG

# DAY 349: YOU WILL MAKE THE NEXT ONE.

My son was shooting the basketball but for whatever reason he kept missing.

I saw his frustration, but each time he missed I kept saying, *"You'll make the next one."*

At first, he looked at me with frustration but then one went in. After one went in he looked at me with confidence and his entire demeanor changed.

He then made like 7 shots in a row. Now him making 7 shots in a row started way before the first one went in. It started when I spoke out loud and he heard, *"You'll make the next one."*

What am I telling you? The exact same thing. You will make the next one. Whatever you are going after just count the basket even before the ball goes in!

You got this! We have 11 days left before you accomplish a goal you set almost a year ago.

These next 11 days I am going to stretch you like never before so get ready to take action!

**TAKEAWAY:** Shoot the shot. Wayne Gretzky said, *"You*

miss 100% of the shots you don't take."

#OGHBYRG

# DAY 350: SHOOT THE SHOT!

I had a dream some time back about me playing in a basketball game. I mean the game was jam packed to the point where it was standing room only.

My team was down by 2 points and I got the ball with 7 seconds left to go in the game. I got the ball at the top of the 3-point line and I was wide open. Nobody was close enough to even contest the shot. But guess what? I never took the shot.

In my dream, time expired with the ball still in my hands. The crowd boo'd me so bad and all my teammates were shaking their heads in disbelief. I get back to the locker room and my teammate said, *"Why didn't you shoot the shot?"* Then he expressed to me how I was one of the best shooters on the team.

As I woke up from this dream, I was so sad. I mean to the point where it felt like it really happened. I began to think about what opportunities have been available to me and I was afraid to, *"take the shot."* I made up in my mind from that day forward, that I would go for it. From now on I'd go for it. No matter how afraid or worried or uncomfortable I may be, I will go! I will shoot the shot!

What shots have you not taken? What opportunities await

you, but you are missing because you won't take the shot? Listen, you got this! You have put the work and effort into it, now just go for it.

**TAKEAWAY:** I told you on yesterday what Wayne Gretzky said, *"You miss 100% of the shots you don't take."* So, shoot the shot.

#OGHBYRG

## DAY 351: GROWTH PROMISES A BETTER TOMORROW.

Hey family, if you want a better tomorrow then you must grow today!

How do I grow, you might ask? I recommend first getting in an environment conducive to growth.

Who are you associating with? Who do you talk to the most? Who is excited for you when you make the right choices and who says, *"you're acting different,"* when you stop making bad choices?

These are things you must look for. When I look at growth, I look at it from all areas and at all levels. I believe the moment you stop growing is the moment that you stop living. I am not trying to be all deep, but I am trying to help you grow.

Remember that growth does not just happen, you must be intentional.

Let's get to it family, and remember you've come way too far to turn back now.

**TAKEAWAY:** The more you grow the higher you will go.

#OGHBYRG

# DAY 352: START!

If you have been reading this book everyday you might be saying, *"What do you mean, start?"*

You have all the tools that you need, you have information that can and will change your life for the better and everything connected with you, but if you do not start then nothing happens.

So, start.

Everything happens with just one step. The one step starts the process. What are you waiting on? You have been missing out on all the great things that are stored up for you. Those that depend on you have been missing out as well. Today is the day that you start!

Do me a favor, tell the 5 people closest to you what you are about to start and why. Making something public adds the accountability factor.

I would like to give advice on some steps to help you make that first step and fulfill your destiny.

**TAKEAWAY:** *"It's never too late to be what you might have been."* – George Elliot

#OGHBYRG

## DAY 353:
## MAKE EVERYDAY WINSDAY!

Look how far we have come. You may not see it but everyone around you can see such a big difference in you.

Your attitude, your thought process, your body, your behavior. You are better because you made the choice to be the best that you can be. You decided not to settle. You decided to get the best out of life that you possibly can, and I am so proud of you for that.

I know this journey has not been easy and there were times that you wanted to quit. Wanting to quit and quitting are two totally different things.

So here we are with 11 days remaining. That's right 11 days remaining until you have completed your 365 days. The goal for this book was never to get you to follow the world's calendar year, but it was to get you to commit to finishing something! Not only finishing something but finishing strong!

Here is your next challenge. Make everyday Winsday. Please pay close attention to the spelling. Winsday not Wednesday.

Wednesdays are known as hump day, but to OGHBYRG nation everyday is hump day and everyday we win! We get over. We overcome. When you go to work and someone says, *"How's your Monday (or whatever day of the week it is) going,"* simply tell them, I don't have Mondays in my week. Only Winsday.

**TAKEAWAY:** *"All I do is win."* – DJ Khaled

#OGHBYRG

# DAY 354:.
# THE 4 C'S

Commit

These next 4 days are critical! Whatever you do, take this and share it with everyone you know that is trying to achieve a greater goal.

Today's C that we will discuss is commitment. You must do this C first in order for the others to work.

Many people think they need confidence to start something, but the reality is you must commit first. Commit means to carry into action deliberately. I have heard people say, "I am going to lose weight," and they truly have that intention. They build the confidence and develop verbal affirmations that this is their year to lose the weight. Guess what happens next?

A couple weeks go by or even months. When they don't see the results they want right away, they revert back to their old ways. They stop eating healthy and stop exercising. This happens because they did not commit to a goal. That is not commitment.

Commitment means that regardless of the highs or the lows, I am going to hang in their until I accomplish my goal. For example, "I weigh 225 pounds and I am going to stick to my diet and exercise plan for as long as necessary to reach my desired weight of 190 pounds." Now once you truly commit to that, there's nothing that can stop you from reaching that goal.

**TAKEAWAY:** Don't talk about it, be about it. Commit. See you tomorrow for your 2nd C.

#OGHBYRG

# DAY 355: THE 4 C'S

Courage

Yesterday we talked about commitment.

After you commit you will develop courage. Courage is not that you will never be afraid or nervous, but even with the nerves, you still will go for it. That's courage.

When you truly commit you develop a sense of courage because you had to take a big step just to commit.

You have so many people depending on you to be courageous! Your courage is giving them courage. Whatever you set your mind to do, it is already done. Just have the courage to step out and go for it.

**TAKEAWAY:** *"It takes courage to grow up and become who you really are."* – E.E. Cummings

#OGHBYRG

# DAY 356: THE 4 C'S

Capability

Today I want you to realize that because you committed and developed the courage to go after being a better you or reaching your dream, now it is time to go to another level within.

Because of the efforts you have made, you are capable. What does this mean? This means you now have the power! That's what capability is, it is power!

Think about it for a moment. When you realize that you can do whatever it is that you are trying to do or achieve, it is a certain kind of mentality that you feel. You feel that you can do anything!

Look at all the greats. There was a moment in their lives where they committed, developed courage and at some point, realized that they were capable.

This applies to you. You got this! You have been given the capability, but you did not realize it because you never committed. Now that you have, the sky is the limit!

**TAKEAWAY:** *"Most of us are capable of more than we believe."* – Nathaniel Branden, Six Pillars of Self-esteem

#OGHBYRG

# DAY 357: THE 4 C'S

Confidence

Here we are. Look at you. Look at the confidence that you now have. I need you to understand that you did not just get here suddenly.

You did not just luck up and something good just so happen to fall in your lap. No! You worked your butt off! You were intentional. You intentionally committed to become a better you 356 days ago.

Next you developed courage along the way. This is what allowed you to keep going and never quit. You may have stopped but you did not quit. I am so proud of you.

Then you realized that you had the capability all along. Now confidence is all over you. Over your brow, your expression, it's even in your smile; no not cockiness but confidence.

Confidence does not look down on others. Confidence seeks for ways to pick others up. Everything connected with you now and in the future will be better because you now understand the 4c's.

Keep up the good work and know that your best is still yet to come.

**TAKEAWAY:** *"I am confident because I actually put the*

*work in."* – Marlon Lock

#OGHBYRG

## DAY 358:
# OGHBYRG

These last 8 days will be near and dear to my heart. All the other days are important as well but let me explain why these last 8 mean so much.

Back in 1974 OGHBYRG was birthed! Let me share with you what OGHBYRG stands for. It's the acronym for:

Obey

God

He'll

Bless

You

Real

Good

My grandparents who founded the church that I now pastor, Unity Gospel House of Prayer, made OGHBYRG the motto of the church. After every service we do a call and response of this. For me, it is a constant reminder that if we obey God, He'll bless us real good.

These next 7 days I will break down each word. I want this motto to be in your skin and come out of your pores. This is something that I live by each and every day of my life.

Every decision I make for myself, my family and my ministry, I make sure that I am obeying God's direction. Proverbs 3:6 says, "In all your ways acknowledge him and he will direct your paths."

In everything that I do, I want to make sure that I am following God's will. I am obeying God.

By doing this I know that I will always have God's blessing and I will always fulfill the purpose that He has for me. I never want to do anything that does not align with God's will. Get ready for a 7-day journey that will cause your life to never be the same. I am so proud of you! You have come so far in such a short amount of time. After the next 7 days you will reach heights you could only imagine. Get some rest and see you tomorrow.

**TAKEAWAY:** *"A solid foundation sets up a solid future."*
– Marlon Lock

#OGHBYRG

## DAY 359: O.G.H.B.Y.R.G.

**The O**

The "O" stands for obey. This speaks volumes to me because it's something that I was taught as a child. In the Bible in the book of Ephesians 6:1 it says, *"Children obey your parents in the Lord for this is right."*

From a child I understood that obedience was right.

We are supposed to obey the laws of the land. Laws add structure to everything. With no laws the world would be horrible. I mean let's be honest, with laws it is still tough. Imagine a society without any laws.

There is another set of laws. That's right, Gods laws, and He requires us to obey them. God does not force us but requires us to obey His laws if we say that we are followers of Him. Basically, if you say that God is in control of your life, then let Him have full control.

I challenge you in this next level of life that you are about to enter, to you humble yourself and obey the laws that are put in place. If you can be faithful over a few things, then God will make you ruler over many.

**TAKEAWAY:** Obedience always leads to a blessing.

#OGHBYRG

# DAY 360:
# O.G.H.B.Y.R.G.

The G

The *"G"* stands for God. The creator of everything. From the beginning it was God. I mean just that alone on a resume is pretty impressive!

To know that we have a God that loves us unconditionally. A God that loves us so much that He gave His only son that we, yes we, may have a right to eternal life. Ok, I just got super excited.

Just think about that for a moment. What I also love about God is that He can always be everywhere. No matter who calls on him, even all at the same time, He is there!

I also love the names of God. Let's look at some…

He's Jehovah – Yireh *"the Lord will provide"*

Genesis 22:13-14

He's Jehovah – Raphe *"the Lord that heals"*

Exodus 15:26

He's Jehovah – Nissi *"the Lord our banner"*

Exodus 17:8-15

He's Jehovah – Shalom *"The Lord our peace"*

Judges 6:24

He's Jehovah – Ra ah *"the Lord is the way, my shepherd "*

Psalms 23:1

Whatever we need God to be whenever we need – He can, if you will (allow).

**TAKEAWAY:** Let God be your source and live the best life you could ever imagine!

#OGHBYRG

# DAY 361: O.G.H.B.Y.R.G.

## The H

The *"H"* stands for He'll, as in when you obey God, He will make a way.

He will be a shelter in times of storm.

He will be a comforter.

He will mend your broken heart.

He will be a yes

He will be a no, until you are ready for the yes.

He will give you hope and a future.

He will provide protection from seen and unseen danger.

Whatever you need God to be in your life, He will be that very thing! It all starts with the obey. Now please know that we all obey something. We obey the good voice, or we obey the bad voice. Which voice have you been obeying?

Make sure you choose wisely. Remember whatever you need God to be and whenever you need Him to be that. Just know He will, you must believe that He IS! He is what? He is God and then He will reward you for seeking His heart (what He cares about) and not His hand (what He can provide).

**TAKEAWAY:** *"He will never leave you nor forsake you."*
– Hebrews 13:5

#OGHBYRG

# DAY 362:
# O.G.H.B.Y.R.G.

The B

The *"B"* stands for bless! That's right God wants to bless each and every one of us. He looks forward to blessing His children.

We must want His blessings. Not His things, but His blessings. Most people equate the blessings of God with things. The Bible clearly teaches how to receive things. In St. Matthew 6:33 it says, *"But seek first the kingdom of God and his righteousness and all these things shall be added unto you."* This simply means that if we seek God first and how to live right according to His word, the things will be added automatically!

I am not talking about things, I am talking about blessings! Blessings are what money cannot afford. Blessings are love, joy, peace, health and strength to name a few. You want these. These are what the world is missing out on.

People think blessings are in things, every time they lose a thing, they become depressed. There are 7,487 promises of God, says Mike Shreve in his book, 25 Powerful Promises of God. Listen! I made up in my mind that everyday I am expecting one. What about you?

**TAKEAWAY:** Say this out loud, *"I am blessed by the best and the best is God."*

#OGHBYRG

## DAY 363:
## O.G.H.B.Y.R.G.

The Y

The "Y" stands for you! You should be excited! Today is all about you and how God wants to bless you.

Almost a year ago, you set out on this journey to be a better you. Not just a better you but the best you that you can be. You have tapped into your purpose. You have become intentional. You think differently. You see the value in you and added value to you. Now that value you have added to you is adding value to everyone and everything connected with you.

I need you to take a moment and celebrate your past.

Celebrate all the not so good that you had to endure, and you overcame.

Celebrate where you are right now.

You have come this far by faith. That's right, you believed that you could but then you grabbed faith and put it into action! Now celebrate your future, because where you are headed is about to blow your mind!

This is a bittersweet day. Bitter, because our journey will end. Sweet, because a new one will begin. See you tomorrow friend.

**TAKEAWAY:** If this book helped you in any way, please recommend someone else to get their copy.

#OGHBYRG

## DAY 364:
## O.G.H.B.Y.R.G.

The R

The *"R"* stands for real. I need you to know that everything that I have shared with you in this book is real and from my heart. So many people have helped me in so many ways and I owe them credit but most importantly God.

When I was at the lowest point in my life God's love reached way down, cradled me, held me, comforted me and established my direction. God used my grandparents to do this. It brings tears to my eyes to I think about how much they loved me, all while I was heading in the wrong direction. Let me explain.

It is easy to love someone that has it all the way right, but they loved me when I had it all the way wrong! That is real love.

They instilled in me that the love of Jesus Christ was real and that all I had to do was confess (or tell) to God that I needed His help and wanted to be saved from my destructive behavior. Then I sincerely asked Him (God) to forgive me of all my sins. God did just that!

The love God showed my grandparents is the same love they showed me and now I am showing you.

Can I be honest and really transparent? When I was writing this book, at first I was concerned about how non-believers would respond to me being a pastor. I thought about how they would view a book that talked about Jesus Christ and would people want to read or promote it. But the more I wrote, the more confident I became in knowing that God was leading me to spread the gospel or the good news of Jesus Christ.

I mean let's be honest. All that I have is because of Jesus! How and why would I not want to share that? I will boldly confess Him all the days of my life! What He has done for me spiritually and the life He has allowed me to live... I would be a fool not to let the world know!

I believe that this book can help you in your business, marriage, finances, and personal life; but once you know that God is real and the love He has for you is real, this book will change your world!

**TAKEAWAY:** Don't be a skeptic, find out for yourself that Jesus is real. Need help? Reach out to me and I, or one of my team OGHBYRG members, will get back in touch with you.

#OGHBYRG

# DAY 365:
# O.G.H.B.Y.R.G.

The G

The *"G"* is for good.

I want to share a verse with you. Psalms 100:5 it says, *"For the Lord is good; his mercy is everlasting; and his truth endureth to all generations."*

Now please read that again but read it slow.

We are not good. There is no good in us except what the Lord places within us. We were all born in sin and shaped in iniquity. That means all we knew to do was sin until we were taught how to live right. So never think that you are good. The Lord is good - that is why we need Him.

Then the verse in Psalms says that His mercy is everlasting. What is mercy? It is the compassion or forgiveness shown towards someone when it is within a person's power to punish or harm. This is what the Lord God did for you and for me. He gave us mercy instead of what we deserved.

His mercy is everlasting which means it never fails!

His truth endures to all generations.

Do you see what happens when you give your life to God? Can't you see how everything about you and connected with you can and will change for the better?

You took a chance on this book. It may have been the cover or the color of the book. It may simply be that you thought it would be a good read. It could have even been because you heard about it or saw an ad. It could be to see what I was writing about and if it is of any value. But the real reason you got this book is because it was ordained by God for you to.

We all are given assignments everyday. Your assignment is connected to someone else; someone you may already be connected with or will be connected with very soon. That person needs you to help them get through what you have already been through. This book was just a set-up to get you back on track or to keep you on track and push you even farther.

I thank you for joining me on this journey. This is our last and final stop. Until we meet again whether it is on this side or the other, I love you with the love of the Lord and there is nothing that you can do about it.

**TAKEAWAY:** Always remember, obey God and He'll bless you real good.

#OGHBYRG

# REFERENCES

Unless otherwise indicated, all Scripture quotations are from the King James Version (KJV).

Bible, King James Version (KJV)

Bible, New Living Translation (NLT)

Bible, New International Version (NIV)

1) Shreve, Mike. *25 Powerful Promises from God*
2) Meriam-Webster.com. 2018. https://www.merriam-webster.com (15 Nov 2018)
3) Maxwell, C. John. *15 Invaluable Laws of Growth*
4) Sinek, Simon. *Together is Better*
5) Tracy, Brian. *No Excuses!*
6) Sullivan, Dan. *The 4 C's Formula: Commitment Courage Capability and Confidence.*
7) Tracy, Bryan. *Eat That Frog.*
8) Yager, Dexter, Mason, John. *The Pursuit. Success is Hidden in the Journey.*

# ACKNOWLEDGMENTS

I want to thank my beautiful wife, Kimberly Lock, who is my best friend and the greatest support system that I could ever have. I want to thank my 5 children: Tone'y you are my oldest but will always be my baby girl. To India you are so smart and intelligent. Whatever you aspire to do you will achieve it. To Asia you will always be my spicy girl and your gift will make room for you. To Sydney (my twin) thanks for being my prayer partner. Souls will be saved because of your commitment to God. To my only son, Marlon 2, I cannot wait to see you take over and run the family business. You will be one of the greatest leaders in the world! I speak blessings over each one of your lives.

To my mother, I have never met a woman as strong as you. Thank you for your strength, it taught me how to be strong.

To my dad, I know you left me at an early age. I look just like you and that makes me feel like you are still here.

To my brothers and sister, I love you. To Mike, you are the best big brother anyone could ask for. Just continue to hold your peace, God's fighting your battle. See you soon.

To my grandparents/parents that stepped in to help my mom raise me and my brothers... words cannot express the impact that you had on my life and still have to this day. Thank you for seeing in me what I never saw in myself. I love you both so much.

To my UGHOP family, you all are the greatest church family in the world! Thank you all for putting up with me and being on this journey called life with me. I am who I am because of you all.

# ABOUT THE AUTHOR

Marlon Lock graduated from the Milwaukee Police Academy, and served as a Police Officer for 5 years, until he resigned to be the Assistant Pastor of Unity Gospel House of Prayer.

On April 8, 2009, Marlon Lock became the Pastor of Unity Gospel House of Prayer, in lieu of the passing of his beloved grandfather, Elbridge Lock (who founded Unity Gospel House of Prayer in 1973).

Marlon is also an accomplished Gospel music artist. In May 2015, He released his debut album Good Seed Project which was nominated in 2 categories of the 2016 Stellar Awards show. Since then Marlon has shared the stage with many renown Gospel Artists and has released other musical projects including his 2017 EP Unleashed and a 2018 single entitled Faith Down to the Ground which features singer and Pastor, Bishop Darrell Hines.

In 2017, Marlon Lock became a certified health and wellness life coach through the Health Coach Institute.

Marlon cherishes being a dedicated husband to his wife Kimberly R. Lock, a published author, who plays a vital role in the ministry and operation of the church. Sharing in their joy are five beautiful children.

Regardless of the platform given, Marlon Lock continues to

promote the unadulterated word of God, lead God's people and impart into all, that if you *"Obey God, He will bless you real good!"* (OGHBYRG, pronounced: AWG-BERG).

www.ingramcontent.com/pod-product-compliance
Lightning Source LLC
Chambersburg PA
CBHW030106240426
43661CB00001B/32